The Macat Library
世界思想宝库钥匙丛书

解析道格拉斯·麦格雷戈

《企业的人性面》

AN ANALYSIS OF

DOUGLAS MCGREGOR'S

THE HUMAN SIDE OF ENTERPRISE

Stoyan Stoyanov　Monique Diderich ◎ 著

童妍◎译

上海外语教育出版社
外教社 SHANGHAI FOREIGN LANGUAGE EDUCATION PRESS

目　录

CONTENTS

引言

要 点

- 道格拉斯·麦格雷戈（1906—1964）成长于20世纪初，正值青年的他亲眼目睹了人们在被称为"经济大萧条"*的全球金融危机中寻找工作所经历的挣扎。

- 通过研究不同组织对员工的管理方式，他提出了一种名为Y理论*的全新管理风格，其基本观点是：人是自我激励的且不需要被严格管控。

- 麦格雷戈的《企业的人性面》（1960）是20世纪最具影响力的管理类书籍之一。

道格拉斯·麦格雷戈其人

《企业的人性面》（1960）的作者道格拉斯·麦格雷戈1906年出生于美国密歇根州底特律市。在他成长过程中，恰逢美国经济大萧条时期（1929年美国股市崩溃后的十年，期间全球数百万人失业、贫困交加）。他发现，即使人们有工作，工资往往也难以负担食宿。在此期间，麦格雷戈有幸进入其家族的慈善机构工作，从而认识了许多生活贫困、挣扎谋生、养家糊口的人。所有这些经历极大地影响了他的职业发展，也激发了他对研究人们最佳工作状态的兴趣。

1935年，麦格雷戈取得哈佛大学的心理学博士学位。他在哈佛大学短暂执教后任教于著名的麻省理工学院（MIT）。麦格雷戈是一名专注于工作条件及员工幸福感的组织心理学家*——即系统研究工作场所对人类心理的影响的人。同时他还研究如何改善工作条件能让员工更加满意。

麦格雷戈生活在一个企业面临巨大变革的时代。他曾目睹了许多大型企业和组织的兴起，以及不断涌现的各种技术创新。这些创新让企业极大地提高了产品的生产，而且也极大地影响了企业对员工的要求。他将观察结果加以总结、分析，1960 年正式出版了《企业的人性面》。但仅仅四年后，他因心脏病发作而突然辞世，享年 58 岁。

《企业的人性面》的主要内容

麦格雷戈在书中写到，管理者看待员工的方式决定了管理风格。他特别比较了两种观点，即 X 理论 * 和 Y 理论，并描述了两种理论是如何影响效率和生产率的。

X 理论是传统的管理理论，其基本观点是人类天性懒散，没有回报就不愿意努力工作。依麦格雷戈来看，具有 X 理论心态的管理者信奉控制员工的严格措施并依赖于奖惩制度：员工工作良好则获得奖励，表现较差则受到惩罚。这种方法不考虑信任在人际关系中的重要性。

相比之下，Y 理论认为员工有目标，并试图将其目标与组织的目标结合起来。这意味着员工与管理层合作以共同实现企业的成功。

Y 理论还假设个人工作不仅是为了满足基本需要：他们也想与同事建立社会关系及友情。因此，读者应当看出这种方法基于人文主义 *，一种重视个人的学习并发挥其创造性潜能之愿望的思想体系。

不同于 X 理论，Y 理论是以美国心理学家亚伯拉罕·马斯洛 * 的 "需求层次" * 理论为基础建立的。马斯洛的理论探讨人类如何被赞誉和学习愿望所鞭策的行为模式。麦格雷戈认为，员工能够学习并以其工作为荣时，工作业绩会更好。他相信对工作满意的员工工作效率会更高，他还提倡员工与管理层相互协作。如果某些组织打算放弃受 X 理论影响的管理风格而采用受 Y 理论影响的管理风格，《企业的人性面》就是他们的行动指南。

麦格雷戈希望藉由本书激励管理者反思其对人类行为的假设以及此类假设如何影响他们与员工的互动关系，并向他们展示如何制定目标以提高员工满意度。他还希望以此激励管理学家建立更加契合现代企业发展的理论。

《企业的人性面》的学术价值

麦格雷戈对优秀管理者采用何种方法激励其员工对雇主的目标产生兴趣（而不是仅仅关心所获得的薪水）进行了研究。他还建议优秀的管理者应该更好地理解人类行为的驱动因素。

麦格雷戈还调查了许多同时代的、有关对待员工之方式的假设。例如，他主张某一组织生产力低下或不盈利时不应该将责任归咎于个体员工。按照麦格雷戈的 Y 理论，管理者对于未满足其员工的特定需要应承担责任。管理者还应负责其员工的职业成长和学习。

麦格雷戈的写作风格清晰而动人，让非学术读者（例如工商界管理者）都可以理解 Y 理论的现实意义。《企业的人性面》也是一份指导手册：麦格雷戈用了一百多页的篇幅描述企业的组织机构应如何开始按照 Y 理论的假设行事。

采用麦格雷戈的 Y 理论的组织经常被称为学习型组织 *，这是因为此类组织能够帮助员工学习和成长，从而实现组织转型。这些组织通常重视自我超越、共同愿景、团队学习。同样的，麦格雷戈的著作也为其逝世后形成的权变理论 * 奠定了基础。权变理论描述了管理层和领导层根据所处市场的状况如何随机应变。

　　《企业的人性面》是麦格雷戈生平最重要的著作。时至今日，该作品仍是有史以来最具影响力的管理学书籍之一。

第一部分：学术渊源

1 作者生平与历史背景

要点

- 《企业的人性面》被美国管理学会（著名的《美国管理学会学报》的出版商）评为 20 世纪最重要的著作之一。

- 麦格雷戈青年时代在其家族的麦格雷戈学院*工作，该机构为失业者和贫苦民众提供援助。

- 他在麦格雷戈学院的工作经历激励他投身于帮助贫民的事业。

为什么要读这部著作？

在《企业的人性面》（1960）一书中，道格拉斯·麦格雷戈介绍了他对现代工作条件的设想。他将这种设想与更传统的员工管理方式进行比较，认为他的人文主义*方法（一种重视人的体验的方法）将产生更有力、更高效的管理实践。

麦格雷戈指出，将员工视为本性懒惰、需要加以严格控制的管理风格不能准确反映人的行为和动机。他认为管理学研究者应该更多地借鉴社会科学领域的研究成果："我和我的一些同事坚信，就企业的人性面而言，社会科学对管理领域的发展应作出比目前情况大得多的贡献。"[1]

他还强调，管理者本身应当了解人类行为相关知识的进展。正如他所说，"职业经理人没必要成为科学家，但他必须见多识广，能够适当运用科学知识。"[2]

麦格雷戈相信员工天生热诚工作，渴望发挥才能，恪尽职守，以期工作做出成绩，满足其自我实现的需要。社会科学的研究成果表明人类渴望成长与学习，基于这一研究成果，麦格雷戈提倡发展一种让管理者将员工视为人力资源的新型管理理论。

麦格雷戈认为，当管理者意识到员工的成长需要时，会鼓励员工为了整个组织的利益而学习、参与组织活动。遗憾的是，当时的雇主并不以这种方法对待员工。正如麦格雷戈所述，"企业组织、指导、控制人力资源的常规管理策略适合于孩子而非成人的能力和特点。"[3]

麦格雷戈成功地提出并捍卫其理念，很快被公认为组织发展*（致力于理解和管理公司、企业等大型组织的变化与发展方式的学术研究）领域中最具影响力的思想家之一。《企业的人性面》已成为后世学者的重要参考书，至今已被引用多达 10 000 次。

> "每个管理决策或行为的背后均是对人类本性和人类行为的假设。"
>
> —— 道格拉斯·麦格雷戈，《企业的人性面》

作者生平

麦格雷戈于 1906 年出生于密歇根州底特律市。青年时代曾在麦格雷戈学院*工作，这是一家由其祖父于 1895 年创立的慈善组织。该学院致力于为难以找到工作的人或虽有工作但收入无法维持生计的人提供帮助，不仅每年为 1 000 多人提供食物和住所，还提供就业指导和宗教支持。麦格雷戈在该学院工作期间逐渐注意到劳动人民所面临的各种问题。

麦格雷戈曾就读于底特律城市学院（现为韦恩州立大学）以及俄亥俄州的欧柏林学院。随后赴哈佛大学攻读心理学，并于 1935 年取得博士学位。他在哈佛大学工作两年后，受聘于麻省理工学院，成为该大学第一位专门研究社会心理学（研究社会背景下思维的运行方式的科学领域）的教师。[4]

除了麻省理工学院的教学工作，麦格雷戈还在一家橡胶密封剂公司担任顾问。他不仅协助公司进行合同谈判、训练工头，还负责处理投诉并就组织的结构化事项提供建议。这样的经历有助于他在实践中不断检验并运用其理论。

1948 年，麦格雷戈任安第奥克学院校长，这是一所位于俄亥俄州耶洛斯普林斯的开明大学，也是最早接受非裔美国学生的美国主流大学之一。六年后，麦格雷戈回到麻省理工学院，成为斯隆管理学院的教师。[5]正是在麻省理工学院的这段教学生涯中，麦格雷戈于 20 世纪 50 年代晚期到 60 年代早期帮助创立了组织发展学这一学术领域。[6]1964 年，也就是《企业的人性面》出版后的第四年，麦格雷戈因心脏病发作与世长辞。

创作背景

麦格雷戈成长于底特律市，该城市后来成为美国最大的工业中心之一、世界汽车之都。[7]在其童年时代，流水线生产方式开始被投入工厂使用。流水线促成了商品的大量生产，对企业产生了巨大影响。流水线改变了工作的性质，工人不再一次制造一辆车，而是被分配特定任务，该任务仅涉及车辆生产的一小部分。

麦格雷戈的职业生涯也受到了 20 世纪 30 年代经济大萧条 * 的影响，这场严重的金融危机导致数百万人失业并陷入贫困。在经济大萧条早期，麦格雷戈在其家族的慈善机构工作，为外来务工者提供临时的食宿。[8]麦格雷戈后来指出，大萧条时代打零工者和失业者艰难度日，而"管理（也）面临严峻的压力。"[9]

　　麦格雷戈与父亲感情甚笃，其父也参与了麦格雷戈学院的事务。父子俩一直保持书信往来，共同探讨人生哲学。尽管父子俩均富有同情心，但麦格雷戈比父亲更加坚信人类的善良天性。

1. 道格拉斯·麦格雷戈：《企业的人性面》，纽约：麦格劳-希尔公司，1960年，第5页。
2. 麦格雷戈：《企业的人性面》，第5页。
3. 麦格雷戈：《企业的人性面》，第43页。
4. 麻省理工学院斯隆管理学院，"麻省理工学院斯隆管理学院的先驱们"，登录日期2015年11月19日，http://mitsloan.mit.edu/faculty/spotlight/pioneered.php。
5. Managers-Net，"道格拉斯·麦格雷戈"，登录日期2015年11月19日，www.managers-net.com/Biography/mcgregor.html。
6. 麻省理工学院斯隆管理学院，"麻省理工学院斯隆管理学院的先驱们"。
7. 麦格雷戈基金会，"历史"，登录日期2015年11月19日，www.mcgregorfund.org/about-us/history。
8. Managers-Net，"道格拉斯·麦格雷戈"。
9. 麦格雷戈：《企业的人性面》，第46页。

2 学术背景

要点 🔑

- 传统上，工业管理的主要方法受科学管理*（一种建立在员工可按照科学路线加以管理之假设的方法）原则的影响。

- 任何企业的工作条件均取决于管理者对于人类天性以及员工激励因素的假设。

- 1954 年，非盈利组织斯隆基金会*（该基金会提供科技教育与研究方面的补助金）提供的一份补助金使得麦格雷戈及其同事有机会系统研究优秀管理者的构成要素。

著作语境

道格拉斯·麦格雷戈在《企业的人性面》中对当时关于管理技术的一般看法做出回应。在 20 世纪早期，管理者对员工实行严格管控，监督他们做什么、如何做、何时做。员工的奖惩取决于他们的工作表现，表现不好可能会被解雇。

麦格雷戈注意到，管理者往往也要接受更高级管理层的仔细审查。例如许多大公司要求管理者接受年度体检，而体检结果决定管理者的职业未来——是否升职。[1]麦格雷戈认为此举表明公司对普通员工和管理者均采取过于严格的控制。

在这种形势下，20 世纪 30—40 年代的美国社会更关注管理政策措施中的道德部分。有关童工、雇佣女工、员工补偿以及集体谈判权（工人可自行组织起来与雇主进行集体谈判）等方面的重要法规得到审议并通过。这些限制条件使管理者不能随意对员工实施控制，通常被管理者视为不合理规定，但最终改善了工作条件。到了20世纪50年代，员工待遇得以提高，而雇主们也越来越多地关注何种工作条件可以提高员工的工作满意度。[2]

> "古典组织理论受制于'民族优越感'：这一理论忽视了政治、社会及经济环境在形成组织、影响管理实践方面的重要意义。"
>
> ——道格拉斯·麦格雷戈，《企业的人性面》

学科概览

20世纪早期的工厂管理实践深受19世纪工程师弗雷德里克·温斯洛·泰勒*提出的科学管理理论的影响。许多同时代的企业都坚定地奉行泰勒关于管理、控制及工作组织的理念。

泰勒的管理理论的一个重要方面是工人应该充分发挥最高的效率，从而创造更大的产量。泰勒研究工厂工人，使用秒表记录他们完成某一特定任务所需的时间。他认为应当按照生产效率最高的工人制定工作标准。

尤其是当像流水线这样的技术创新得到应用，工人开始执行小件、重复性的任务时，以这种标准来要求工人成为企业广泛采用的做法。按照泰勒的预测，提高工人的生产效率可以为公司创造更高的利润，员工也可以获得更高的工资。

泰勒的理论基于"人类天生具有一种松懈的天性，也可称作'本性磨洋工'*"这一信念。[3]他认为，一个人工作缓慢会导致其他本来努力的同事也同样慢悠悠地工作，泰勒将这种现象称为"系统磨洋工"*。系统磨洋工给生产率带来消极的影响，降低企业

13

的利润。

学术渊源

麦格雷戈接受过系统的心理学培训，这促使他吸收其他心理学家在群体动力学 *（该领域研究人们在群体中的行为）方面的研究成果，这一研究领域始发于 20 世纪 30 年代。德裔美国心理学家库尔特·勒温 *是群体动力学领域中一位极负盛名的人物，他主要研究领导力以及领导力如何影响群体绩效。按照企业发展顾问安东尼·勒纳 *的观点，勒温及其同事"不仅受到求知欲的引导，更有一种紧迫感，想要更好地理解促成民主制度及个人在社会参与中所做选择的群体行为要素。"[4]

麦格雷戈还受麻省理工学院的学术氛围所影响。20 世纪 50 年代初，在麻省理工学院工业管理学院顾问委员会的一次会议中，富有的汽车企业总裁阿尔弗雷德·斯隆提出了若干个有关成功经理人的问题，这些问题激励麦格雷戈开始从事对多种管理风格的系统化研究。1954 年，他获得了非盈利机构斯隆基金会的一笔补助金，从而保障了该项研究的持续进行。

麦格雷戈还受到其他同事的影响，比如管理学者西奥多·阿尔弗雷德 *（也是麦格雷戈所带的一位研究生）。他们走访了多名经理人，[5] 这一合作研究为《企业的人性面》奠定了基础。麦格雷戈很有可能曾与亚历克斯·巴弗拉斯 *（美国心理学家及企业管理教授，也是麻省理工学院的一名教师）分享了相关知识。

1. 道格拉斯·麦格雷戈:《企业的人性面》,纽约:麦格劳-希尔公司,1960年,第13页。

2. 麦格雷戈:《企业的人性面》,第12页。

3. 弗雷德里克·温斯洛·泰勒:"科学管理原理",艾米·S.沃顿编,《在美国工作:连续性、冲突与变化》,加利福尼亚州山景城:梅菲尔德出版公司,1998年,第67—75页。

4. 亚瑟·勒纳:"麦格雷戈的遗产:关于他的学术影响、理论及尚待探索问题的思考",《管理史杂志》第17卷,2011年第2期,第219页。

5. 麦格雷戈:《企业的人性面》,第 v 页。

3 主导命题

要点 ⚿

- 管理者对于人类行为的假设决定了其对待下属的行为方式。

- 20 世纪早期至中期的传统管理风格是以对人类行为的错误理解为基础的。

- 传统的组织理论既未体现当时对技术的理解，亦未体现对人类行为的社会科学研究成果。

核心问题

在麻省理工学院工业管理学院顾问委员会的一次会议中，企业家阿尔弗雷德·斯隆提出了两个对于麦格雷戈而言非常重要的问题：怎样才能成为一位成功的管理者？"成功的管理者是天生的，还是后天培养的？"[1]

1954 年，麦格雷戈在斯隆基金会*（一家旨在支持创新科技研究与教育的组织）的资助下，继续研究这些问题。他仔细审视了各种大公司举办的经理培训项目，从而"更深入地了解各种理论与实践如何影响不同组织中管理者的培养。"[2]该项研究也试图确定哪种类型的人有能力成为管理者以及管理者采取何种方式能够鼓励员工学习、成长。

麦格雷戈在日常生活中不断研究管理者的实际活动，他还观察这些管理者与其上级、下属的各种互动。他发现管理者对人类行为的假设极大地影响了其与下属的互动。

由此，他系统地研究了高级管理者针对"最有效的员工管理方法"所持有的假设。[3]

麦格雷戈的著作涉及四个核心问题：

- 优秀管理者具有哪些要素？
- 管理者对于人类天性持有何种假设？
- 这些假设是否正确？
- 社会科学的最新进展是否在组织中得到运用？

> "如果存在一个传统组织理论共有的假设，那就是：权威是管理控制中核心的、必不可少的手段。这是教科书式管理理论中基本的组织原则。组织的结构就是权威关系的等级制度。"
>
> ——道格拉斯·麦格雷戈，《企业的人性面》

参与者

道格拉斯·麦格雷戈是人文主义*管理学（一种重视个人成长与学习的思想体系）的倡导者。他曾受到诸如库尔特·勒温*（在 20 世纪 30 年代研究群体动力学*）等心理学家的启发。他还吸收了其他学者的研究成果，如社会工作者玛丽·派克·福莱特*（组织行为学先驱）、澳大利亚心理学家埃尔顿·梅奥*（专门从事群体动力学研究）以及心理学家亚伯拉罕·马斯洛*（曾提出马斯洛需求层次理论这一著名人类行为模型）。[4]

麦格雷戈从梅奥处习得：工人重视团队归属感甚于金钱报酬，工人的满意度依赖于工作环境中的合作与社交。换言之，在梅奥看来，对社交方面感到满意的工人具有更高的生产效率。[5]

麦格雷戈的理论基础来自亚伯拉罕·马斯洛的《人类动机的理

论》，该书描述了马斯洛需求层次理论和自我实现 *（发展创造性潜能的个人欲望）的概念。⁶ 麦格雷戈将其关于"管理者应对人类行为持什么看法"的观点建立在马斯洛需求层次理论上。

马斯洛理论把人类需求分为不同层次。最底层的是生理需求，即对食物和住所的需求。其上一层是安全需求，即对安全的生活、工作环境的需求。随后是社会需求，即对良性人际关系和有意义的工作的需求。接下来是自尊需求，即与自尊、自信有关的需求。处于需求层次顶端的是自我实现需求，即发挥个人的能力到最大程度，充分实现个人创造性潜能的需求。

尽管传统的管理策略仅关心生理需求和安全需求（两种最低层次的需求），麦格雷戈建议管理层还应努力满足更高层次的需求，只有这样做才能改善工作满意度，从而提高生产效率。

同期争议

20 世纪初期，在社会科学界曾发生过一次有关"组织理论之未来"的重要讨论。古典理论学家采纳西格蒙德·弗洛伊德 *（被誉为精神分析学 * 之父）的观点，后者认为人类天性懒散，如果不加以控制和激励则不愿意努力工作。⁷ 这与行为管理学 *（该领域的先驱为美国心理学家约翰·华生 *、B. F. 斯金纳 *）领域的研究结论相左。*⁸ 行为管理学理论家认为，管理实践应满足人类的成长、学习需求。

战后时期 *，即第二次世界大战结束后数百万士兵返回家园的调整期，研究者趁此机会研究如何建立组织结构并管理员工。在这段时期，麦格雷戈和其他倡导行为管理学的学者向主张工人需要严格管控的科学管理 * 理论发起了挑战。

　　包括麦格雷戈在内的行为管理学家以及企业管理顾问彼得·德鲁克将人文主义价值观念运用于管理实践以及组织领导学。麦格雷戈从心理学角度出发批判古典管理原则，他大量引入心理学概念，将人类动机和行为运用于员工发展研究，还探索如何在最大程度上运用社会科学的相关知识进行组织管理。

---

1. 道格拉斯·麦格雷戈：《企业的人性面》，纽约：麦格劳-希尔公司，1960年，第v页。
2. 麦格雷戈：《企业的人性面》，第vi页。
3. 麦格雷戈：《企业的人性面》，第vii页。
4. 亚伯拉罕·马斯洛："人类动机的理论"，《心理学评论》，1943年第50期：第370—396页；亚伯拉罕·马斯洛：《动机与人格》，纽约：哈珀与罗出版公司，1954年。
5. Managers-Net："乔治·埃尔顿·梅奥"，登录日期2015年11月20日，www.managers-net.com/Biography/Mayo.html。
6. 马斯洛："人类动机的理论"，第370—396页。
7. 西格蒙德·弗洛伊德："精神分析纲要"，《国际精神分析期刊》，1940年第21期，第27—84页。
8. 约翰·华生："行为主义者视角中的心理学"，《心理学评论》，1913年第20期，第158—177页。

4 作者贡献

要点 ⛌━

- 麦格雷戈专注于对当时的管理风格及其在组织中的效用进行系统分析。

- 麦格雷戈尝试引导管理人员从心理学角度理解人类的行为动机。

- 他相信这些全新的心理学理解可以构成新的管理策略和实践的基础。

作者目标

作为《企业的人性面》的作者，道格拉斯·麦格雷戈终其整个职业生涯，努力探究组织运营及建立结构的复杂方式。他还试图确认是否能设计出一种工作条件，既能实现公司目标又能满足员工个人需求。此前，人们一直认为权威、层级以及控制是激励员工工作的关键因素，却不赞同视员工为资源的观点，不愿接受心理学家研究发现的有关人类动机的基本原则。

麦格雷戈力证，基于对人类行为的过时观点形成的传统管理策略阻碍了工作效率和生产力的提高。谈及这些策略，他写道："责怪员工未能按照预期行事，这并不能提高管理水平。"[1] 换言之，当传统管理实践未能达成预期效果，公司不应该把过错归咎于员工。

除了吸纳心理学相关理论外，麦格雷戈还想要开发出一种根植于人文主义 *（一种重视人类个性，强调发挥个体潜能的思想体系）的管理理论。

麦格雷戈的理论有助于企业从现代化的视角建立组织结构，看待员工。不仅如此，他还进一步强调，加强员工人文关怀不仅能增强员工满意度，更能提高生产效率。

> "读者应能了解我的看法：我们现在认为应该行之有效的管理方法，其实还远远不够。"
>
> —— 道格拉斯·麦格雷戈，《企业的人性面》

研究方法

麦格雷戈的研究方法包括对组织的管理风格进行分析。他系统地研究了组织环境中盛行的、有关人类行为的各种假设，他尤其想证明，那些遵从西格蒙德·弗洛伊德*的著作以及早期管理学者弗雷德里克·温斯洛·泰勒*的"科学"理论中关于人类行为的观点的组织，并没有给员工营造出一个有利于提高效益、效率以及生产力的工作环境，自然也就不能充分发挥其人力资源的潜能。

麦格雷戈确信心理学、社会科学研究有利于开发更有效的管理方法，这些方法对雇主和员工双方都有益。他引用组织理论家、工业研究者埃尔顿·梅奥*以及心理学家亚伯拉罕·马斯洛*的著作，说明在团队中工作会让人们更快乐，生产效率更高。

纵观《企业的人性面》全书，麦格雷戈始终认为，管理者应仔细检验自己对人类行为的假设如何影响他们对待下属的方式。麦格雷戈以其独到的见解帮助组织创造更舒适、高效的工作条件，确保组织全员顺利发展。

时代贡献

麦格雷戈是历史上最早对传统的员工监管方式提出质疑的管

理学家之一，他主张管理者调适自己对人类能力的固有看法。即使在这一观点盛行之后，麦格雷戈的著作仍然在众多同类作品中脱颖而出。他不仅能够融会贯通众多领域的杰出研究成果，还能切中要害，深入浅出。

麦格雷戈在《企业的人性面》中描述了两种主要的管理理论，即 X 理论*和 Y 理论*。X 理论（即传统的一般看法）假定人天性懒散，需要采取严格控制、依据绩效奖惩的方法。与之相对的 Y 理论则认为，人们不仅想体验财务增长，更想体验能力提高和情感认同。麦格雷戈主张现代企业将组织实践的管理思想从 X 理论转移到 Y 理论。

麦格雷戈认为，管理者采取新的管理方法前应考虑其自身风格以及对人性的看法，这一点尤为重要。X 理论体现了对于人类动机的消极观点。践行传统的管理者在工作中并没有激发员工的主观能动性*（员工不需要管理者给出指示即可启动项目的能力）和信任感。正如麦格雷戈所述，"人们如果在工作期间的各种重要需求得不到满足与尊重，就会以各种可预期的行为来对付工作，也就是磨洋工、消极被动、不愿承担责任、拒绝改变……（以及）要求获得不合理的奖励。如此看来我们似乎在作茧自缚。"[2] 他认为 X 理论管理实践会导致员工缺乏满足感，从而使生产效率下降。

麦格雷戈倡导的管理方式，即 Y 理论，试图与埃尔顿·梅奥发现的人们喜欢群体性工作这一现象以及亚伯拉罕·马斯洛的需求层次理论*（描述一系列人类行为之动机的心理学模型）相契合。麦格雷戈写道，"除非工作能满足员工这些高层次的需求，否则他们将会产生被剥夺感，而其行为也将体现这种被剥夺感。"[3]

麦格雷戈认为，为了避免产生被剥夺感，需要让员工感受到他们的工作是有意义的，他们不仅在群体关系中收获了尊重和友谊，还从学习和协作中获得精神的满足。

最重要的是，企业应如何实现工作条件的现代化对于研究组织发展*（一门研究大型组织如企业和机构如何发展、演化的学科）的学者而言是重中之重，麦格雷戈不仅提出问题，更就这一问题提出了宝贵见解，引人深思。

---

1. 道格拉斯·麦格雷戈：《企业的人性面》，纽约：麦格劳-希尔公司，1960 年，第 11 页。
2. 麦格雷戈：《企业的人性面》，第 42 页。
3. 麦格雷戈：《企业的人性面》，第 40 页。

第二部分：学术思想

5 思想主脉

要点 &—

- 被麦格雷戈称为 X 理论 * 的古典组织理论是基于关于人类行为及动机的错误假设。

- X 理论的奖惩制度会产生适得其反的效果。

- 麦格雷戈提出的替代方案，即他所称的 Y 理论 *，可帮助管理者设计有利于员工自尊、身份及自我实现的工作条件。*

核心主题

在《企业的人性面》一书中，道格拉斯·麦格雷戈区分了两种不同的管理方法，即其所称的 X 理论和 Y 理论，并分别说明两者如何塑造组织的文化。他希望通过这种比较来证明 Y 理论更有利于员工及雇主。对于更加人性化的 *Y 理论如何对企业更有助益，他还作出了理论解释。

麦格雷戈写道，X 理论是以激励为基础的，"激励的逻辑是人们想赚钱，他们更加努力工作是为了赚更多钱。"[1] 按照 X 理论，只要能获得金钱奖励，人们愿意接受严格的控制。

然而，该书着重指出这一理论是基于对人类天性的误解。X 理论体系无法创造高产的、符合要求的工作条件，因为该体系未考虑到其他众多影响人类行为的重要因素，而是假定人类天性懒散。正如麦格雷戈所述，"X 理论为管理者提供了针对组织绩效低下的合理借口：这是我们手头的人力资源的天性使然。"[2]

> "只有当我们认识到控制表现为有选择性地适应人类天性，而非试图让人类天性符合我们的意愿之时，才能够提高我们的控制能力。"
>
> ——道格拉斯·麦格雷戈，《企业的人性面》

思想探究

麦格雷戈指出了 X 理论所持的三种有关人类行为的主要假设：

"普通人天生厌恶工作，能躲则躲。"[3]

"由于人类具有这种厌恶工作的特性，大多数人必须在受逼迫、受控制、受指示或以惩罚相胁的情况下，才会全力实现组织目标。"[4]

"普通人更愿意接受指示，不愿意承担责任，他们缺乏上进心，而且更渴望安全感。"[5]

如果人们只有在受逼迫、受控制的情况下才工作，则可通过奖惩制度进行管理。麦格雷戈将这种制度称之为"胡萝卜加大棒"的员工激励。按照 X 理论，员工将只会为了金钱之类的激励（"胡萝卜"）而工作，并且会努力避免受罚或被解雇（"大棒"）。

当人们须努力工作以获取基本必需品（如食物、住所）时，"胡萝卜加大棒"的制度会相当奏效。麦格雷戈也提到，确实，管理者可以通过满足或压制这些需求来控制员工。"当面包很少时，人们常常仅为了面包而活。"[6]

此外，麦格雷戈认为，工作本身应该具有激励性。如果工作的唯一好处是获得工资用于日常花销，那么工作就像一种惩罚：员工只是为了以后过上好日子而去工作。这样会产生问题，因为正如麦格雷戈所说，公司将"几乎无法指望员工接受超过限度的此种惩罚（指工作）。"[7]

因此，麦格雷戈认为，工作本身应该能够让人产生满足感：工作应该具有意义，能够满足自尊需求。他建议采取一种能够满足这些另外的"高层次"需求的方法，作为 X 理论的替代方案。他将这种方法称为 Y 理论，该理论的基本假设源自心理学家亚伯拉罕·马斯洛 * 和埃尔顿·梅奥 * 的心理学研究成果。

Y 理论的主要假设如下：

"（人们）在努力实现其所希望达到的目标过程中会进行自我引导和自我控制。"[8]

"普通人在适当的条件下不仅学会接受责任，而且学会主动承担责任。"[9]

"有较高而非较低比例的人具有以较高水平解决组织问题的想象力、谋略和创造性。"[10]

"在现代工业生活的条件下，普通人的智力潜能仅有一部分得到利用。"[11]

Y 理论的假设是：员工可以在职场获得成长和发展，而管理层应当开发人力资源的潜能，有选择地根据个体员工调整其管理策略。除了对工作中学会新技能必须予以奖励之外，Y 理论还认为员工具有"与其名誉相关的需求：对身份的需求、对认可的需求、对欣赏的需求、对同事给予的应有尊重的需求。"[12]通过这种方式，Y 理论引入了当代的人类行为理念，以让管理实践与时俱进。

语言表述

麦格雷戈希望他的理论对管理科学学术界和现实的企业管理均产生影响。因此，《企业的人性面》旨在启发学者以及工商界人士。[13]麦格雷戈能够利用其在一家橡胶及密封剂公司担任顾问的经历，与学术界以外的读者产生共鸣。

　　麦格雷戈被公认为组织发展 * 领域最重要的贡献者之一。由于他希望作品易于管理者理解，该书中的若干章节可用作任何工商企业实施 Y 理论的指导手册。《企业的人性面》对管理学界以及商界均产生了巨大的影响。

---

1. 道格拉斯·麦格雷戈：《企业的人性面》，纽约：麦格劳-希尔公司，1960 年，第 9 页。

2. 麦格雷戈：《企业的人性面》，第 48 页。

3. 麦格雷戈：《企业的人性面》，第 33 页。

4. 麦格雷戈：《企业的人性面》，第 34 页。

5. 麦格雷戈：《企业的人性面》，第 34 页。

6. 麦格雷戈：《企业的人性面》，第 41 页。

7. 麦格雷戈：《企业的人性面》，第 40 页。

8. 麦格雷戈：《企业的人性面》，第 47 页。

9. 麦格雷戈：《企业的人性面》，第 48 页。

10. 麦格雷戈：《企业的人性面》，第 48 页。

11. 麦格雷戈：《企业的人性面》，第 48 页。

12. 麦格雷戈：《企业的人性面》，第 38 页。

13. 彼得·韦尔："新时代的过程智慧"，ReVISION 第 7 卷，1986 年第 2 期，第 39—49 页。

6 思想支脉

要点

- 麦格雷戈 Y 理论*的一个局限在于很难评估工人绩效：当员工实施自我管理时，应如何确定加薪幅度？

- 麦格雷戈推荐采用斯坎伦计划*，该计划由炼钢工人兼地方工会主席约瑟夫·斯坎伦*于 20 世纪 30 年代提出。斯坎伦计划的依据是员工参与以及成本节约分享*（员工享有公司利润分成）。

- Y 理论针对管理者的目标至今仍未广泛实现，是因为公司并未致力于促进员工的学习和成长。

其他思想

《企业的人性面》一书中一个关键的次要观点是道格拉斯·麦格雷戈对如何改变绩效评审以体现 Y 理论之假设这一问题的探索。根据一个学术分析报告的说法，麦格雷戈所处时代的绩效评审"大多按照与 X 理论一致的方式实施。换言之，这些评审为单向评审且清晰体现了一种由监督者、管理者及组织所实施的外部控制方法。"[1] 麦格雷戈指出，改变员工评价方式可以在积极方向上重塑整个组织。

麦格雷戈介绍了一种评估方法，其特点是不同组织层级之间进行对话（尤其是低级、高级管理者与其员工之间的对话）以形成合作。麦格雷戈提倡将员工目标与公司目标实现同步。他认为，绩效评审不应导致奖励或惩罚，而应鼓励各级员工共同参与，以改善公司业绩。

> "如果上司告知下属其面临的问题并向下属寻求最佳的解决方案，那么就会促成更高的参与度。"
>
> —— 道格拉斯·麦格雷戈，《企业的人性面》

思想探究

麦格雷戈认为，员工应对其任务和职责具有更多的控制权，而这些职责应与组织的总体目标保持一致。这种管理办法由管理顾问彼得·德鲁克*在其著作《管理实践》（1954）中首次提出，现在通常称为"目标管理（MBO）"*。

麦格雷戈以德鲁克的方法为基础，重点研究如何在组织内部建立关系。他认为，绩效评审应基于这些关系所带来的成果，而非仅基于个人绩效。[2] 这样就形成了人性化的组织结构，该结构重视个体员工的成长和发展，并运用了行为管理学的知识。

麦格雷戈也是斯坎伦计划的倡导者，该计划以炼钢工人及工会会员约瑟夫·斯坎伦的名字命名（工会是一个旨在确保更好的工作条件或报酬的工人组织）。斯坎伦计划是一种聚焦于成本节约分享和有效参与的管理哲学，与 Y 理论的原则相一致。[3]

按照麦格雷戈的说法，成本节约分享是指员工分享"组织绩效改善"带来的经济收益。[4] 除工资外，员工还能获得月度奖金，奖金额度取决于整个组织的产量。这样有助于他们"发现其个人行为与组织绩效之间的关联性"。[5] 换言之，通过这种安排，他们能体会到其个人成功与公司整体的成功密切相关。

斯坎伦计划的另一方面，即有效参与，指建立委员会，让员工召开简短的头脑风暴会议（即自发产生并讨论各种想法）。麦格雷戈指出，通过这种方式，公司获得"具有显著经济效益的创意"，无需外部顾问提供服务。这两项原则，即成本节约分享和有效参与，还可以改善生产现场（员工工作的物理空间）中员工之间的关系。

被忽视之处

自 1960 年出版以来，《企业的人性面》已被一代又一代学者深入探讨。然而，工商界尚未真正采用促进员工自我实现*（员工实现其全部创造性潜能的机会）的管理模式。

麦格雷戈认为，如果企业能够促进自我实现和人文价值，员工满意度将会提升，因而企业能够在效率和生产力方面取得更好的业绩。这样还会产生更低的工作流动率，从而降低雇佣、培训新员工的成本。就职场文化以及员工需求方面的假设而言，麦格雷戈认为，如果完全采用 Y 理论，该理论将成为自我实现的预言。[6]

然而，时至今日，各类组织尚未"提供自我实现的机会"。[7]原因之一是，较之麦格雷戈写作《企业的人性面》的时代，如今员工更换工作的频率已大幅提高了。因此，各类组织已逐渐重新考虑在员工发展方面的投入（包括自我实现的机会）。[8]

---

1. 彼得·索伦森和马特·米纳汉："麦格雷戈的遗作：Y 理论管理的演化与现代应用"，《管理史杂志》第 17 卷，2011 年第 2 期，第 178—192 页。
2. 理查德·巴布科克："目标管理（MBO）历史溯源"，载《目标管理的战略与战

术》，理查德·巴布科克和彼得·索伦森编，伊利诺伊州香槟市：斯台普斯出版社，1976年，第2—24页。

3. 商业词典："斯坎伦计划"，登录日期2015年11月20日，www.businessdictionary.com/definition/scanlon-plan.html。

4. 道格拉斯·麦格雷戈：《企业的人性面》，纽约：麦格劳-希尔公司，1960年，第111页。

5. 麦格雷戈：《企业的人性面》，第112页。

6. 索伦森和米纳汉："麦格雷戈的遗作"。

7. 托马斯·海德："道格拉斯·麦格雷戈的遗作：获得的教训和遗失的教训"，《管理史杂志》第17卷，2011年第2期，第202—216页。

8. 伦西斯·利克特：《人的组织：其管理与价值》，纽约：麦格劳-希尔公司，1967年。

7 历史成就

要点 🔑

- 《企业的人性面》最初是一篇同名的论文。[1]

- 麦格雷戈告诫说，X 理论 *（其基础假设是工人是懒惰的，仅在受到严格控制或为获得金钱激励的情况下才会工作）实践主导的环境不利于实施 Y 理论 *实践。

- 麦格雷戈承认，运用 Y 理论较费时，因为许多组织长期采用 X 理论管理策略。

观点评价

尽管道格拉斯·麦格雷戈的《企业的人性面》重点关注 X 理论管理是如何控制员工（尤其是通过逼迫和惩罚），他也承认 X 理论的某些方法比其他方法更加细腻。某些管理者比较宽容，比如说专注于满足员工的需求，以实现工作场所的和谐状态。麦格雷戈指出，其实这种更加细腻的方法也是另一种控制形式，与更严格的策略一样不利于生产；这意味着员工可能想得到更多、付出更少。

麦格雷戈宣称，无论采用哪一种 X 理论管理风格，其结果均是公司无法实现其经济目标。X 理论实践也无法创造有利于人们顺利发展的工作条件，因为这些实践仅满足生理需求（与食物、住所有关的需求）和安全需求（在没有危险的环境中工作的愿望）。

另一方面，按照 Y 理论策略，管理者可以灵活满足其员工的社会需求（与协作和归属感有关的需求）以及自我需求（包括自信、独立、成就、知识、欣赏、身份和认可）。然后，组织可以努力满足其员工的自我实现*需求。[2]

麦格雷戈认为，管理者抛弃其关于员工的限制性假设（X 理论所确定的假设）比接受 Y 理论的假设更重要。[3]然而，他的确希望管理者能够通过各种实践，来满足其员工的各种不同需求。因此，Y 理论的重要意义在于，该理论是 X 理论的替代性方案，而麦格雷戈并未将其视为唯一的有效方法。

> "我们常常认为老板毕竟是老板。实际情况并非如此。由于管理者从事不同的活动，情况每天乃至每时每刻都在变化，因而相应的影响方式也随之改变。"
>
> —— 道格拉斯·麦格雷戈，《企业的人性面》

当时的成就

麦格雷戈当时正以经理们为研究对象，当他首次向经理们介绍其理论（即古典管理理论基于对人类行为的错误假设）时，就很高兴地发现"越来越多的管理者意识到现有方法的不足之处。"随后他将该研究结果与其在麻省理工学院工业管理学院的同事分享。

通过这种方式，麦格雷戈从他的研究对象以及同事那里获得了对于其观点的反馈。这些反馈促使他撰文，标题为《企业的人性面》，并于 1957 年出版。他的 X、Y 理论引发了管理学者们的讨论。这些讨论帮助他不断完善观点，最终以最成熟的形式呈现在《企业的人性面》一书中。

当他的著作首次出版时，管理者们乐于接受从 X 理论到 Y 理论目标的转变。麦格雷戈认为，企业若不能满足马斯洛需求层次*中所述的员工需求，则无法提高其生产力和效率。这一观点大受欢迎。

麦格雷戈的 X 理论和 Y 理论引发了组织发展 * 学界对心理学和管理学的大量研究。此外，他的观点也被其他学术领域所采纳，同时影响了这些学术领域的发展，其中包括组织行为学、领导力、战略学以及人力资源管理（对员工、技能、雇佣政策等的管理）。

局限性

麦格雷戈本人是第一个承认 Y 理论的局限性的人，他写道，"诸如 Y 理论的假设这样的理论假设，必然包含一些实践中不可能实现的条件。"[5] 他并未将此视为"障碍"，而是将其视为"发明与发现的动力"。[6]

麦格雷戈还意识到，有些组织会发现采用 Y 理论的假设更容易，而其他一些组织则不然。对于一些长期采用 X 理论实践的组织而言，做出这种转变虽说并不是完全不可能，但至少是相当困难的：管理风格的重大变化需要对结构、职能部门乃至所雇佣的管理者类型进行彻底改革。

即便如此，麦格雷戈详细描述了企业如何能够在短时间内运用 Y 理论。他深入分析了各种组织理论，以期引发学者及工商界人士的讨论。他的著作提倡在业内人力资源方面进行协作。[7]

---

1. 道格拉斯·麦格雷戈："企业的人性面"，1957 年 4 月 9 日首次发表在《思想与行动的探险》（即剑桥市麻省理工学院工业管理学院五周年大会论文集），马

萨诸塞州剑桥市：麻省理工学院工业管理学院，1957；重印于《管理学评论》，1957 年第 46 期，第 22—28 页。

2. 道格拉斯·麦格雷戈：《企业的人性面》，纽约：麦格劳-希尔公司，1960 年，第 38 页。

3. 麦格雷戈：《企业的人性面》，第 245 页。

4. 麦格雷戈：《企业的人性面》，第 245 页。

5. 麦格雷戈：《企业的人性面》，第 245 页。

6. 麦格雷戈：《企业的人性面》，第 246 页。

7. 麦格雷戈：《企业的人性面》，第 246 页。

8 著作地位

要点 &

- 麦格雷戈在其职业生涯中致力于研究管理风格与员工效率的关系。《企业的人性面》是其最具影响力的学术著作。

- 他认为缺乏创新、效率低下与 X 理论 * 实践有关。

- 麦格雷戈的各类著作在整个 20 世纪具有重要意义。

定位

　　道格拉斯·麦格雷戈的《企业的人性面》介绍了其在整个职业生涯中分析管理风格所获得的各种见解；他关注垂直管理 * 关系（管理者与下属之间的关系）的重要性，将其视为对工作条件影响最大的因素。麦格雷戈是一位坚定的人道主义者 *，认为应尊重员工并为其提供成长机会。

　　按照组织理论家丹尼尔·卡茨 * 及罗伯特·卡恩 * 所述，麦格雷戈的 Y 理论 * 采用 "参照权力"（基于喜欢或认同某人而产生的影响力）。[1] 麦格雷戈提倡员工与管理者之间相互协作、共同参与管理，认为这样会增进彼此关系。卡茨和卡恩认为，如果所有员工能够相互协作、共同参与管理，整个组织将会更加高效。[2]

　　麦格雷戈将 Y 理论视为可以实现最高员工满意度、最高生产效率的管理风格。按照彼得·圣吉 *（管理理论家、麻省理工学院高级讲师）的说法，麦格雷戈解释了由 X 理论主导的公司很难创新的原因，但 Y 理论也未必能确保创新。[3]

　　不幸的是，麦格雷戈于《企业的人性面》发表之后第四年逝世，没来得及解答圣吉等人所关心的问题。

> "本书的目的不是要求管理者在 X 理论、Y 理论之间选择其一。更确切地说，其目的是鼓励大家意识到理论的重要性，并促使管理者仔细审查其假设并加以明确化。这样才能打开通往未来的大门。"
>
> ——道格拉斯·麦格雷戈，《企业的人性面》

整合

麦格雷戈在批判 X 理论的管理实践时同时指出，当代的管理实践已经"明显减少了经济困境，消除了各种形式的工业战争，提供了基本安全、舒适的工作环境，但并未改变其基本的管理理论。"[4] 换言之，尽管 X 理论管理满足了基本需求，但并未进一步改变工作条件。如果各类组织能够改变其有关对待员工方式的假设，生产效率还可以进一步提升。

但并非所有人都同意麦格雷戈的观点。他的主张均基于管理者与其下属之间的关系中产生的心理相互作用。因此，批评者认为，麦格雷戈未考虑到环境因素，比如企业所处的文化氛围，或者政府调控下的经济、法律影响。他们认为，这些因素也会影响组织并降低效率。[5]

一些公司也拒绝接受麦格雷戈的如下观点：高管人员应就停滞不前的生产效率承担最大的责任。

意义

麦格雷戈引领了同时代的理论需求和思潮。其理论的提出促进了企业结构建设及管理方式的现代化。其著作的重要性在于将心理学概念与管理概念结合起来，从而鼓励管理者自我反思，并以更人性化的方式对待员工。

总而言之，麦格雷戈的著作在组织管理学界大受欢迎，其大名也在管理学教材中屡被提及。实际上，根据《经济学人》杂志于1993年所做的一项民意调查，麦格雷戈是史上最受欢迎的管理学者。[6]

《企业的人性面》一书也颇受欢迎，被美国管理学会（声誉卓著的《美国管理学会学报》的出版者）评选为20世纪最重要管理学著作第四名。该书于2011年被《时代》杂志评为"25本最具影响力的工商管理图书"之一。[7]

1. 丹尼尔·卡茨和罗伯特·卡恩：《组织中的社会心理学》，纽约：约翰·威利父子出版社，1966年，第302页。

2. 卡茨和卡恩：《组织中的社会心理学》，第303页。

3. 彼得·圣吉："创新实践"，《领导人对话》，1998年第9期，第16—22页。

4. 道格拉斯·麦格雷戈：《企业的人性面》，纽约：麦格劳-希尔公司，1960年，第46页。

5. 沃伦·本尼斯："正确看待麦格主席"，《管理史杂志》第17卷，2011年第2期，第1-11页。

6. 蒂姆·欣德尔：《管理思想与大师指南》，伦敦：侧影出版社，2008年。

7. "25本最具影响力的工商管理图书"，《时代》，登录日期2015年11月20日，http://content.time.com/time/specials/packages/completelist/0,29569, 2086680,00.html。

第三部分：学术影响

9 最初反响

要点 🔑━━

- 《企业的人性面》于 1960 年首次出版时便受到学术界的广泛关注。
- 麦格雷戈受到了支持传统管理风格的人士的批评。
- 有些人认为麦格雷戈的 Y 理论 * 曲解了人性。

批评

道格拉斯·麦格雷戈在《企业的人性面》一书中对 X 理论 * 的批评本身受到了那些支持传统管理技术的人士的批评。他们指责麦格雷戈对人性持有"扭曲的"观点。[1] 具体来说,他们认为:人类在不同的环境下表现不同;职场行为不同于家庭行为或社群行为。

此外,即使麦格雷戈的用词温和且客观,他的人道主义 * 价值观还是引发了批评。尽管知名心理学家亚伯拉罕·马斯洛的 * 需求层次理论 * 为 Y 理论奠定了坚实的基础,但 Y 理论有其自身的局限,这意味着,麦格雷戈的著作同样有局限。事实上,马斯洛本人也是麦格雷戈的批评者之一,他认为 Y 理论太理想化、不太实用,不能运用于工作场所。[2]

其他批评者,例如麦格雷戈在麻省理工学院的同事艾德加·沙因 *,与马斯洛的看法一致。[3] 沙因认为,尽管 Y 理论对于人类天性的假设符合事实,但管理者没有责任让员工参与决策过程。[4] 因此,他认为 Y 理论应仅适用于高层管理者。[5]

麦格雷戈还因为其获取、解释数据的方式受到批评。有一位学者评述道："麦格雷戈将其论点部分建立在观察形成的模糊印象上，并以一种漫不经心的方式验证其假设。"[6]换言之，麦格雷戈过多关注改善员工的工作条件，却忽视了实施 Y 理论所面临的一些挑战。

> "……权威是当今美国工业界完全依赖的一种不恰当的控制手段……在某些情况下，权威必不可少，但就促进协作而言，权威充其量是一根不牢固的拐杖。"
>
> —— 道格拉斯·麦格雷戈，《企业的人性面》

回应

其他还有一系列更为多样化的反响。例如，荷兰著名的跨文化心理学家*（研究跨文化边界心理学异同点的心理学家）吉尔特·霍夫斯塔德*表示，X 理论和 Y 理论均基于有关人类天性的过于宽泛的假设。尤其是，霍夫斯塔德认为，这些理论均未考虑"规避不确定性"*（人们愿意接受意外事件的程度）在不同的文化之间存在的差异。

依照霍夫斯塔德所述，有些国家的人应对不确定性时准备不足，因此只能对决策施加较小的影响。在此类情况下，X 理论可能比 Y 理论更有效。考虑到这一点，提倡完全摒弃 X 理论实践似乎并不合理。[7]

麦格雷戈的著作也成为其他学者的理论基础，例如管理学者威廉·大内*于 1981 年提出了 Z 理论*。[8]日本工商企业在 20 世纪 70 年代非常成功，因此，大内想通过采纳日本企业的一些特点，来帮助美国建立竞争优势。当时，日本公司提供终身雇佣且关注员工福利，员工士气高昂，企业也获得了经济收益。[9]

冲突与共识

在所有对其作品的质疑中，麦格雷戈觉得尤其有必要回应霍夫斯塔德的批评，即组织所处的文化影响了 X 理论或 Y 理论的作用。霍夫斯塔德敦促麦格雷戈具体说明其理论最适用的环境。[10]

麦格雷戈的同事艾德加·沙因起初为麦格雷戈辩护时表示，X 理论和 Y 理论只不过是描述管理者持有的有关员工的两套不同理念的标签而已。麦格雷戈并非要求所有组织均采取 Y 理论实践，他只是建议将 Y 理论作为可用于替代 X 理论的一项方案。在麦格雷戈《职业经理人》(1967 年在其去世后出版) 一书的引言中，沙因写道，"仅有很少的读者愿意承认麦格雷戈的书秉持中立立场。"[11]

之后运用《企业的人性面》的人都注意对麦格雷戈的观点加以调整，以把文化对工作环境的影响也考虑进去。

1. 哈罗德·格兹考，对罗伯特·坦南鲍姆、欧文·韦施勒以及弗雷德·马萨里克合著的《领导力与组织：一种行为科学方法》的评论，《美国社会学评论》第 26 卷，1961 年第 3 期，第 804 页。
2. 亚伯拉罕·马斯洛：《优心态管理：一份日志》，伊利诺伊州霍姆伍德市：欧文出版社，1965 年。
3. 艾德加·沙因："捍卫 Y 理论"，《组织动力学》，1975 年第 4 期，第 17—30 页。
4. 艾德佳·沙因："性别角色定型与女性管理者所需的管理特征之间的关系"，《应用心理学杂志》第 60 卷，1975 年第 3 期，第 340—344 页。
5. 大卫·雅各布斯："书评：道格拉斯·麦格雷戈《企业的人性面》处于险境"，《管理学会评论》第 29 卷，2004 年第 2 期，第 293—296 页。

6. 雅各布斯："图书评论"，第 294 页。

7. 卡罗尔·桑切斯和道恩·柯蒂斯："不同的心态、共同的问题：吉尔特·霍夫斯塔德对民族文化的研究"，《绩效改进季刊》第 13 卷，2000 年第 2 期，第 9—19 页。

8. 威廉·大内：《Z 理论：美国企业界怎样迎接日本的挑战》，马萨诸塞州雷丁市：艾迪生—卫斯理出版社，1981 年。

9. 思维工具编辑团队："Z 理论：融合东西方的管理风格"，登录日期 2015 年 11 月 24 日，www.mindtools.com/pages/article/theory-z.htm。

10. 沃伦·本尼斯："正确看待麦克主席"，《管理史杂志》第 17 卷，2011 年第 2 期，第 1—11 页。

11. 道格拉斯·麦格雷戈：《职业经理人》，纽约：麦格劳-希尔公司，1967 年，第 11 页。

10 后续争议

要点 🔑━━

- 麦格雷戈成功说服了众多管理者采用 Y 理论 * 原则。

- 麦格雷戈的一些观点与权变理论 * （研究管理及领导实践应如何配合或适应某一市场或文化的理论）结合使用。

- 在《企业的人性面》基础上进行的研究确定了哪些特定情形和文化背景更适用 X 理论或 Y 理论。

应用与问题

道格拉斯·麦格雷戈《企业的人性面》中所述的理论承诺带来成长和效率提升，因此很快被很多公司采用。例如，在跨国消费品公司宝洁，高管们将 Y 理论应用于该公司的一家制造厂。他们尝试实行一种具有如下特点的管理结构：所有员工职衔类似，按照目标管理（MBO*，即由员工制定旨在达成公司目标的详细计划）进行决策，[1] 并定期监测业绩。[2] 最终，这家工厂生产效率提高了 30%。[3]

麦格雷戈认为将亚伯拉罕·马斯洛 * 的需求层次理论 * 运用于工作场所，不仅能促进员工协作和沟通，而且激励员工学习和成长，管理者们普遍认可这一看法。不过，在心理学家吉尔特·霍夫斯塔德 * 提出"X 理论或 Y 理论能否成功适用取决于文化背景"这一批评后，麦格雷戈的理论在学术界就不如在商界那么受追捧了。即便如此，许多学者依然采纳《企业的人性面》所述的理论和观点。

> "有时他（管理者）的角色可能是其许多下属的领导，有时可能是同级别经理人团队中的一员。有时他的角色可能是导师，有时可能是决策者、纪律执行者、助手、顾问，或仅仅是观察者。"
>
> ——道格拉斯·麦格雷戈，《企业的人性面》

思想流派

学者们继续探究 X 理论和 Y 理论的实施如何影响组织适应和学习的方式。例如，基于麦格雷戈的著作，管理理论家彼得·圣吉*创造了"学习型组织"一词，指通过鼓励员工学习而实现自我转型的公司。

学习型组织基于如下观点：不存在所谓的最佳管理方法，而最佳管理者能够适应新环境，并且能够应对不断变化的市场环境。换言之，在某种环境中有效的策略在另一种环境中可能无效。这种观点有时也被称为权变理论，现在有大量证据支持这一观点。[4]

当代研究

如今，研究《企业的人性面》的学者会考虑到霍夫斯塔德关于 X 理论、Y 理论受文化影响的警示。这就开辟了新的研究方向。

例如，英国组织社会学教授琼·伍德沃德*认为，X 理论适用于从事大规模生产的企业，而 Y 理论更适用于制造复杂、高端产品的企业。[5]麦格雷戈在麻省理工学院的同事艾德加·沙因*提出了一种新版的 Y 理论，其并非基于人道主义*原则，而是基于权变理论原则。[6]

其他学者认为，X 理论适用于稳定的环境，而 Y 理论适用于快速变化的环境。[7] 还有一些学者认为，不同的理论可用于同一组织的不同部门：管理者可根据其理念以及部门本身文化，创造不同的工作条件。[8]

一般说来，学者们关注的焦点已不再是将管理风格分为 X 或 Y 以及在组织内部提倡人文价值等事项。[9]

1. 理查德·巴布科克："目标管理（MBO）历史溯源"，载《目标管理的战略与战术》，理查德·巴布科克和彼得·索伦森编，伊利诺伊州香槟市：斯台普斯出版社，1976 年，第 2—24 页。

2. "目标管理"，《经济学人》，登录日期 2015 年 11 月 20 日，www.economist.com/node/14299761。

3. 罗伯特·沃特曼：《卓越的前沿：向以人为本的公司学习》，伦敦：尼古拉斯·布里利出版公司，1994 年。

4. 大卫·雅各布斯："书评：道格拉斯·麦格雷戈《企业的人性面》处于险境"，《管理学会评论》第 29 卷，2004 年第 2 期，第 293—296 页。

5. 琼·伍德沃德：《产业组织：理论与实践》，纽约：牛津大学出版社，1965 年。

6. 艾德加·沙因："性别角色定型与女性管理者所需的管理特点之间的关系"，《应用心理学杂志》第 60 卷，1975 年第 3 期，第 340—344 页。

7. 汤姆·伯恩斯和乔治·斯托克：《创新管理》，伦敦：塔维斯托克，1961 年。

8. 保罗·劳伦斯和杰伊·威廉·洛尔施："三种环境中的高绩效组织"，载《组织与环境：管理差异化和整合》，保罗·劳伦斯和杰伊·威廉·洛尔施编，马萨诸塞州波士顿：哈佛大学商学院出版社，1967 年，第 133—158 页。

9. 达恩·海瑞格尔、苏珊·杰克逊和约翰·斯洛克姆：《管理学：基于能力的方法》，俄亥俄州辛辛那提：西南大学出版社，2002 年。

11 当代印迹

要点 🗝—

- 麦格雷戈想要改变对员工的评估方式。
- 学者提倡组织成为"学习型组织",其特点是能适应不断变化的环境。
- 麦格雷戈继续影响着管理学领域的研究。

地位

在《企业的人性面》一书中,道格拉斯·麦格雷戈认为公司的创新能力是与其管理者评估自身管理风格的能力相关联的,并提出管理者很有必要对其特定管理风格影响员工的方式进行反思。

同样地,他认为,应向员工提供客观反馈,而且管理者不应进行年度绩效评审。他写道,这种评审的问题在于,"评审所提供的行为'反馈'与行为本身有较长的时间间隔。"[1]他还认为,个人不应获得绩效工资,因为此类工资基于管理者的主观判断。

相反,麦格雷戈提议依据团队绩效的客观指标发放团队奖励。团队中绩效最高的员工还可获得一大笔奖金。然而,时至今日,美国企业通常发放个人绩效工资而非团队奖金。

如今,仍有不少学者继续发展麦格雷戈的理论。麦格雷戈说明了管理者必须反思其实践如何影响垂直管理(即管理者与下属)关系*的原因,管理学家彼得·圣吉*对这一观点进行了详细阐述。[2]圣吉指出,如果管理者一直关注实现目标,则很难注意到他们自己对于人类天性的假设。[3]美国的企业理论家克里斯·阿吉里斯*认为，一个组织如果希望成为"学习型组织"，就应建设能够带来创新、创造和高效的工作条件。[4]

> "随着时间的推移，麦格雷戈的观点变得更加有用、更加及时、更加重要。"
>
> ——彼得·德鲁克，收录于苏丹·卡玛里《人员管理大师》

互动

组织行为学家*（即基于"行为有助于深入了解人类心理"这一观点研究组织运行机制的人士）支持麦格雷戈的如下观点：高度控制机制会导致员工变得过于顺从，而这最终会不利于公司发展。组织的领导层应利用其权力在管理者和员工之间创造互惠互利的关系。

自从吉尔特·霍夫斯塔德*指出麦格雷戈的 Y 理论*未考虑文化差异后，学者们已经消除了 X 理论*与 Y 理论之间的严格界限。这表明各个学派支持者之间的讨论中已不再以这些术语定义不同管理类型。相反，新的"权变理论"*将 X 理论和 Y 理论的要素结合起来。通过这种方式，当今的管理理论仍含有麦格雷戈的思想。

最近，有一位学者承认《企业的人性面》对于组织管理学*的价值，但评论说，该书过于关注管理者与其员工之间的心理关系，却可能忽略了整个组织的文化。[5]

持续争议

麦格雷戈《企业的人性面》出版距今已近 50 年，这一著作仍然影响着组织发展*方面的学术文献。[6] 其他学者的著作中频频提及麦格雷戈，可见他对该领域的影响力之大。

在 20 世纪 80 年代，麦格雷戈一直是相关学术研究不可或缺的一部分。2000 年，《再访道格拉斯·麦格雷戈：管理企业的人性面》一书再次引起了人们对其学术著作的兴趣。该书包含了《企业的人性面》的部分节选，书中乐观地预计，未来我们工作的世界将是"麦格雷戈式"的世界。[7]

2004 年，麦格雷戈因倡导提高员工参与度而广受褒奖。正如一位评论者所述，"麦格雷戈的道德观表明（他）认识到管理模式的选择对员工的影响。"[8] 2011 年，《管理史杂志》整整一期都是不同学者关于麦格雷戈的遗作、贡献及局限性的文章。[9] 一位知名的管理学者在文章写到，麦格雷戈已经给商业及管理研究界留下了"不可磨灭的印象"。[10]

由此可见，麦格雷戈的著作仍与当今的研究密切相关。

---

1. 道格拉斯·麦格雷戈：《企业的人性面》，纽约：麦格劳-希尔公司，1960 年，第 87 页。

2. 彼得·圣吉："创新实践"，《领导人对话》，1998 年第 9 期，第 16—22 页。

3. 彼得·圣吉：《第五项修炼：学习型组织的艺术与实践》，纽约：双日出版社，1990 年。

4. 克里斯·阿吉里斯：《教聪明人如何学习》，马萨诸塞州波士顿：哈佛商业出版社，1998 年。

5. 沃伦·本尼斯："正确看待麦克主席"，《管理史杂志》第 17 卷，2011 年第 2 期，第 1—11 页。

6. 沃伦·伯克：《组织变革：理论与实践》，加利福尼亚州千橡市：赛吉出版社，

2008 年；沃伦·伯克："道格拉斯·麦格雷戈的遗作"，《应用行为科学杂志》2009 年第 45 期，第 8—11 页。

7. 加里·赫尔、沃伦·本尼斯和德博拉·斯蒂芬斯：《再访道格拉斯·麦格雷戈：管理企业的人性面》，纽约：威利出版社，2000 年，第 viii 页。

8. 大卫·雅各布斯："书评：道格拉斯·麦格雷戈《企业的人性面》处于险境"，《管理学会评论》第 29 卷，2004 年第 2 期，第 293—296 页。

9. 彼得·索伦森和马特·米纳汉："麦格雷戈的遗作：Y 理论管理的演化与现代应用"，《管理史杂志》第 17 卷，2011 年第 2 期，第 178—192 页。

10. 罗伯特·坎宁安："道格拉斯·麦格雷戈：不可磨灭的印象"，《艾维商业期刊》，2011 年第 75 期，第 5—7 页。

12 未来展望

要点 🔑

- 麦格雷戈的 Y 理论＊至今尚未得到广泛推行的一个原因是，公司通常进行短期规划，这阻碍了它们对员工长期发展进行投资。

- 麦格雷戈的《企业的人性面》对于解释当前的经济趋势（如美国最近的经济衰退）有重要意义。

- X 理论＊指导下的管理可能导致类似于"电子血汗工厂"＊的办公场所。

潜力

尽管道格拉斯·麦格雷戈的《企业的人性面》鼓励公司对其员工的个人成长进行投资，但如今大多数公司的战略规划通常仅仅涉及未来三年内的业务。[1] 由于公司不为员工的未来做长期规划，造成了就业市场不稳定；这种现象还促使人力资源经理宁愿雇佣经过培训的人员，而不愿意花费时间对未经培训的雇员进行培养。[2]

造成上述状况的原因之一是，在人们频繁跳槽的时代，培训员工的成本高昂，而这些成本往往会抵消掉麦格雷戈认为采用 Y 理论实践所带来的生产率提升。即便如此，管理者仍在利用 Y 理论的假设来鼓励创造创新。

"《企业的人性面》未考虑文化差异"这一批评如今依然成立。21 世纪的企业招聘的员工越来越多样化：员工和管理者可能来自各种不同的地区和文化。这意味着不同的部门可能存在不同的组织形式，对不同类型的员工要采用多样化的管理风格。

《企业的人性面》中，正是这一点有望在今后的进一步发展中得到改进。调整其理论以适应多元文化背景，将使其可为当今的企业所用。

> "……他对人类关系的道德视角仍然很有价值，即使情境已经发生改变。实际上，在当今这个充满了公司裁员、养老保障不足以及激进型投资者追求即刻回报的时代，重新考虑麦格雷戈关于'重视员工未发挥的潜能'这一呼声具有重要意义。"
>
> ——大卫·雅各布斯，"书评：
> 道格拉斯·麦格雷戈《企业的人性面》处于险境"

未来方向

美国最近的经济衰退（被称为"大衰退"*）体现了麦格雷戈著作的重要性。这次经济低迷期（2007—2009 年）的特点是失业率升高（从 2007 年的 5% 升至 2009 年的 10%）、工资低、雇佣时间短、工作条件恶化（如不再提供健康保险等附加福利）。³ 数百万美国人谋职求生，希望能够付得起账单、养活家庭。这让我们想起了麦格雷戈的观点，"只要一个人为求生而工作，他就会被控制。当面包不多时，人们往往仅为面包而活。"⁴ 高失业率导致管理层仅关注经济目标，而忽视了员工的工作满意度。

由此导致当今许多公司遵循 X 理论的假设和原则，更有甚者，这些公司如今可以使用与 X 理论方法对应的技术手段，例如通过电脑监控随时监控员工：在现代呼叫中心，员工的电脑屏幕会弹出窗口，提醒他们加快工作速度。这使得有些学者认为，这些科技手段会将办公场所变成"电子血汗工厂"。[5]

结语

在《企业的人性面》一书中，道格拉斯·麦格雷戈比较了两种截然不同的管理类型。按照 X 理论，管理者假定员工想尽可能少工作，因而需要建立严格的控制体系。相比之下，Y 理论认为，员工需要成长、学习、责任感以及创造力，方可成为好员工。麦格雷戈支持 Y 理论，认为该理论可以提高效率和生产力。

麦格雷戈及其追随者的研究最终造就了一种新的关于组织如何运作的思维方式：权变理论*，该理论要求管理者使组织的需求和经济目标适应于组织所在社会的经济和文化状况。公司应运用 Y 理论原则，成为"学习型组织"*，从而适应新的、不断变化的动态市场。

尽管麦格雷戈于 1964 年逝世，但其著作仍然影响着企业组织和管理学者。

1. 托马斯·海德："道格拉斯·麦格雷戈的遗产：获得的教训和遗失的教训"，《管理史杂志》第 17 卷，2011 年第 2 期，第 202—216 页。
2. 威廉·安东尼、米歇尔·卡克马尔和帕梅拉·佩雷威：《人力资源管理：战略方针》，俄亥俄州梅森：汤普森/西南大学出版社，2006 年。
3. 莫妮卡·柯克帕特里克·约翰逊、蕾娜·安贝·赛吉和杰兰·莫蒂默："职业价值观、早期职业生涯困境与美国经济衰退"，《社会心理学季刊》第 75 卷，2012 年第 3 期，第 242—267 页。

4. 道格拉斯·麦格雷戈：《企业的人性面》，纽约：麦格劳–希尔公司，1960年，第41页。

5. 保罗·阿特威尔："老大哥与血汗工厂：自动化办公室里的电脑监控"，《社会学理论卷》，1987年第5期，第87—100页。

术语表

1. **斯隆基金会**：非盈利性机构，由艾尔弗雷德·P. 斯隆于 1934 年创立。斯隆长期担任通用汽车公司总裁，他建立该基金会的目的是对科学技术的创新研究提供资助。

2. **行为管理**：一种强调工作中人的因素的管理类型。行为管理将人视为具有成长潜能的个体资源，也称为人际关系运动。

3. **行为主义**：一种认为人类行为有助于深入了解人类心理，并且可以对人类行为进行测量、训练和改变的理论。

4. **权变理论**：一种管理理论，其基础理念是决策和领导取决于组织所处的运营环境。

5. **成本节约分享**：一种允许员工分享组织成功（例如，产量提高或生产成本降低）所产生的物质奖励的政策。除基本工资外，员工还获得月度奖金。

6. **跨文化心理学**：研究不同文化之间心理学差异与相似性的心理学分支。

7. **电子血汗工厂**：管理层采用电脑监控手段持续监控员工的工作场所。"血汗工厂"一词指其员工受到剥削，工作时间长但工资待遇低的企业。

8. **经济大萧条**：1929 年美国股市暴跌后的十年时期，在这段时期内数百万美国人失业，生活贫困。

9. **大衰退**：2007—2009 年间美国金融市场崩溃，导致数百万美国人失业。在此期间，失业率曾接近 10%。

10. **群体动力学**：研究人类在群体中的行为方式的学科，该词由心理学家库尔特·勒温首次创造。

11. **需求层次理论**：一种由心理学家亚伯拉罕·马斯洛提出的概念，对

人类动机的不同类型进行描述并排序。他发现的"需求金字塔"包括各种需求，从基本的生理需求（对食物和住所的需求）直至对成就和自我实现的需求。

12. **人文主义**：认为个人应有机会实现其全部潜能的哲学体系。从企业的角度而言，人性化的工作条件结合了员工需求和公司目标以取得更高的效率。

13. **学习型组织**：学习型组织的基础理念是不存在所谓的最佳管理方式。在学习型组织中，所有员工具有共同的愿景，聚焦于团队学习，组织能够灵活适应其环境（包括经济、文化环境）。

14. **目标管理（MBO）**：一种管理者和员工共同制定目标和计划的体系。此类计划得到定期监控，以确保没有偏离目标。

15. **麦格雷戈学院**：一家致力于帮助就业困难人士的慈善机构，由道格拉斯·麦格雷戈的祖父于 1895 年创立。

16. **组织行为学家**：采用行为主义假设及方法系统研究组织功能的人士。

17. **组织发展（OD）**：致力于理解、管理组织变革的学术领域。库尔特·勒温通常被视为组织发展学之父。

18. **组织心理学**：一门系统研究工作场所如何影响员工心理的学科。

19. **本性磨洋工**：员工在工作时松懈的倾向。

20. **战后时期**：第二次世界大战之后的调整期，在此期间数百万士兵回归美国，而欧洲则进行战后重建。

21. **精神分析**：一种针对潜意识引起的行为现象和状况的治疗手段和理论研究方法。

22. **参照权力**：由管理学者丹尼尔·卡茨和罗伯特·卡恩创造的术语，用以描述管理者利用其下属的尊敬与拥戴而获得的权力。

23. **斯坎伦计划**：一项由工会会员、炼钢工人约瑟夫·斯坎伦于 20 世纪 30 年代制定的用于帮助企业应对经济形势的计划。该计划要求企业利用员工的潜能，并倡导员工协作。

24. **科学管理**：一种根据科学原则进行组织管理的观念，也被称为"泰勒主义"，以实业家、早期管理学者弗雷德里克·温斯洛·泰勒的名字命名。

25. **自我实现**：一个人发挥其创造性潜力。

26. **主观能动性**：员工不需要管理者的指示而开始工作的能力。

27. **垂直管理关系**：一个描述上级与其员工、下属之间关系的术语。最初指的是管理者与流水线员工的关系。

28. **系统磨洋工**：当一个或多个员工做其工作要求的绝对最小量时，其他员工也开始尽可能少地工作。

29. **X 理论**：一种管理学理论，假设人是天性懒散、厌恶工作，仅在受到严格控制或为获取经济报酬的情况下工作的"实利人"。该理论反映了传统管理原则，其理论基础是西格蒙德·弗洛伊德的精神分析和 F. W. 泰勒的科学管理原则。

30. **Y 理论**：一种管理学理论，假设是人类是自我激励的"自动人"，不需要被严格控制。按照 Y 理论的假设，员工努力工作的目的是学习和成长，工作之后引起自豪，满足其自尊和自我实现的需要。

31. **Z 理论**：日本学者威廉·大内在日本企业的成功经验基础上提出的一种管理学理论。该理论认为，美国企业应吸收东方的管理风格，后者重视员工幸福感等一系列因素。

32. **规避不确定性**：一个特定国家或文化中的人们能够接受意外事件、不确定性或模糊不清状态的程度。这一概念由荷兰跨文化心理学家吉尔特·霍夫斯塔德首次提出。

人名表

1. 西奥多·阿尔弗雷德（1925—2007），位于俄亥俄州克利夫兰市的凯斯西储大学管理与政策学教授。他曾获得麻省理工学院（MIT）工业经济学博士学位，求学期间曾与道格拉斯·麦格雷戈开展合作研究。

2. 克里斯·阿吉里斯（1923—2013），美国企业理论家，哈佛大学商学院教授，专攻组织内部行为研究。

3. 亚历克斯·巴弗拉斯（1920年生），美国心理学家，麻省理工学院（MIT）工商管理教授，曾在麻省理工学院创设了团队网络实验室。

4. 彼得·德鲁克（1909—2005），奥地利裔美国讲师、管理顾问。出版书籍有《公司的概念》（1972）和《管理：使命、责任、实务》（1974）。

5. 玛丽·派克·福莱特（1868—1933），社会工作者、管理理论家，被视为组织理论及组织行为学领域的先驱。

6. 西格蒙德·弗洛伊德（1856—1939），奥地利神经学家，因创立精神分析学（一种通过分析病人的无意识冲突来治疗心理障碍的治疗及理论模型）而享有盛名。

7. 吉尔特·霍夫斯塔德（1928年生），荷兰社会心理学家，主要关注跨文化群体及组织的研究，因提出文化维度理论而享有盛名。

8. 罗伯特·卡恩（1918年生），美国心理学家，专攻组织管理学及调查研究法，与丹尼尔·卡茨合著了《组织社会心理学》（1966年出版）。

9. 丹尼尔·卡茨（1903—1998），美国心理学家、组织心理学专家，曾任密歇根大学教授，因其1966年出版的《组织社会心理学》而闻名于世。

10. 安东尼·勒纳：外部组织发展顾问，亚瑟·勒纳联合公司的负责人之一。

11. 库尔特·勒温（1890—1947），德裔美国心理学家，社会心理学及组织心理学领域的先驱，为群体动力学、组织发展学的研究做出了贡献。

12. 亚伯拉罕·马斯洛（1908—1970），美国心理学家，提出了著名的马斯洛需求层次理论。

13. 埃尔顿·梅奥（1880—1949），澳大利亚心理学家、组织学家、行业研究者，专门研究团队内成员的行为。

14. 威廉·大内（1943年生），加州大学洛杉矶分校安德森商学院的组织与管理教授，因著作《Z理论》（1981）而闻名于世。在该书中，他建议美国企业借鉴东西方管理风格并加以融合，从而相得益彰。

15. 约瑟夫·斯坎伦（1899—1956），美国曼斯菲尔德钢铁厂工人、地方工会主席，曾提出斯坎伦计划，该计划的核心基础是成本节约分享与强调员工参与。曾应道格拉斯·麦格雷戈邀请，担任麻省理工学院讲师。

16. 艾德佳·沙因（1928年生），麻省理工学院前教授、社会心理学家、道格拉斯·麦格雷戈的同事，出版过企业文化方面的著作。

17. 彼得·圣吉（1947年生），管理学家、麻省理工学院管理学院高级讲师，创立了组织学习协会。

18. B.F. 斯金纳（1904—1990），美国心理学家、行为学家，曾任教于哈佛大学，被公认为现代行为主义发展的关键人物。

19. 阿尔弗雷德·P. 斯隆（1875—1966），富有的汽车企业高管，于1952年创建了麻省理工学院的工业管理学院。

20. 弗雷德里克·温斯洛·泰勒（1856—1915），工程师，科学管理的创始人，被管理界誉为科学管理之父。科学管理为古典组织理论奠定了基础。

21. 约翰·华生（1878—1958），美国心理学家，创立了行为主义心理学派。

22. 琼·伍德沃德（1916—1971），英国组织社会学教授，曾任教于伦敦帝国理工学院。

WAYS IN TO THE TEXT

- Douglas McGregor (1906–64) grew up in the early twentieth century. When he was young, he witnessed firsthand the struggle of those searching for work in the worldwide financial crisis known as the Great Depression.*

- Studying the ways in which different organizations manage their employees led him to develop a novel management style, Theory Y,* founded on the idea that people are self-motivated and do not need to be strictly controlled.

- McGregor's *The Human Side of Enterprise* (1960) is one of the most influential books about management of the twentieth century.

Who Was Douglas McGregor?

Douglas McGregor, the author of *The Human Side of Enterprise* (1960), was born in 1906 in Detroit, Michigan, in the United States. Growing up, he witnessed the Great Depression (the decade following the 1929 collapse of the US stock market, which led to unemployment and impoverishment for millions worldwide). He also saw that even when there was employment, wages were not always enough to pay for food and housing. In these years, McGregor had the opportunity to work for his family's charitable organization, where he met people who were living in poverty and struggling to provide for their families. Together, these experiences greatly influenced his career and his interest in the conditions in which people worked best.

In 1935, McGregor received his doctorate in psychology from Harvard University. He then taught briefly at Harvard before eventually becoming a faculty member at the prestigious Massachusetts Institute of Technology (MIT). McGregor's work as an organizational psychologist*—someone engaged in the systematic study of how the workplace affects the human mind— focused on working conditions and employee well-being. He also studied how working conditions could be made more satisfying for workers.

McGregor lived during a period of great change for businesses. He witnessed the emergence of many large enterprises and organizations, and the advent of numerous technical innovations. These innovations allowed corporations to drastically increase their production of goods—and they had a similarly dramatic effect on what was required of workers. His observations eventually led to *The Human Side of Enterprise*, published in 1960. Only four years later, at the relatively young age of 58, he died of a heart attack.

What Does *The Human Side of Enterprise* Say?

In his book, McGregor writes that a management style is based on how managers see their employees. He compares and contrasts two views in particular, which he calls Theory X* and Theory Y, and describes how they influence efficiency and productivity.

Theory X, the traditional theory of management, is based on the belief that human beings are lazy by nature and will not work hard without being rewarded. According to McGregor, managers with a Theory X mind-set believe in strict measures for controlling employees and rely on a system of rewards and punishments: employees receive rewards for good performance and are punished if they work poorly. This approach does not account for the importance of trust in human relationships.

By comparison, Theory Y recognizes that employees have goals, and attempts to integrate these goals with those of the organization. This means that employees work with management toward the success of the enterprise.

Theory Y also assumes that individuals do not work to fulfill basic needs alone: they also want to develop social relationships and camaraderie with their colleagues. For these reasons, readers should see his approach as being rooted in humanism,* a philosophy that values the individual's desire to learn and to fulfill his or her creative potential.

Unlike Theory X, Theory Y builds on the American psychologist Abraham Maslow's* "hierarchy of needs,"* a model of human behavior that describes how people are motivated by praise and the desire to learn. Employees work better, McGregor argues, when they are able to learn and take pride in their work. He believes that satisfied employees are productive employees, and he advocates collaboration between employees and managers. *The Human Side of Enterprise* is a guide for organizations that want to abandon a management style informed by Theory X in favor of one informed by Theory Y.

McGregor hoped that his book would inspire managers to reflect on their assumptions about human behavior and on how those assumptions influence their interactions with employees, and would show them how to set goals that take into account employee satisfaction. He also wanted to inspire academics who study management to build theories that fit modern businesses better.

Why Does *The Human Side of Enterprise* Matter?

McGregor examines how good managers motivate their employees to take an interest in the goals of their employers (rather than concerning themselves with simply receiving a paycheck). He suggests that good managers have a better understanding of what drives human behavior.

McGregor also investigates many contemporary assumptions about how employees should be treated. For example, he argues that individual employees should not be blamed when an organization is unproductive or unprofitable. Under McGregor's Theory Y, the manager is to blame for failing to adapt to their employees' specific needs. Managers are also responsible for their employees' professional growth and learning.

McGregor's writing is clear and engaging, which makes it possible for people other than academics—managers in the business world, for instance—to understand the practical implications of Theory Y. *The Human Side of Enterprise* is also a guide: McGregor devotes more than a hundred pages to describing how organizations can begin to work on Theory Y assumptions.

Organizations that use McGregor's Theory Y are often called learning organizations* because they are able to transform themselves through helping their employees learn and grow. These organizations often value personal mastery, shared vision, and team learning. Similarly, McGregor's work also laid the groundwork for contingency theories* that were developed after his death.

Contingency theories describe how management and leadership must adapt and change depending on the state of the markets in which they operate.

The Human Side of Enterprise was the most important work of McGregor's life. Even today, it remains among the most influential books written on management.

SECTION 1
INFLUENCES

THE AUTHOR AND THE HISTORICAL CONTEXT

KEY POINTS

* *The Human Side of Enterprise* has been declared one of the most significant works of the twentieth century by the Academy of Management, publisher of the highly respected *Academy of Management Journal.*

* When he was young, McGregor worked for his family's McGregor Institute,* a charitable organization that assisted those who were unemployed or disadvantaged.

* His experiences with the McGregor Institute encouraged him to dedicate his career to helping impoverished people.

Why Read This Text?

In *The Human Side of Enterprise* (1960), Douglas McGregor introduces his vision for modern working conditions. He compares this vision to a more traditional way of managing employees, arguing that his humanistic* approach (an approach that values the human experience) will lead to more effective and efficient managerial practices.

According to McGregor, a management style that treats employees as lazy and in need of strict control does not reflect human behavior and motivation accurately. He argues that those who study management should draw more on research from the field of social sciences: "I share with some of my colleagues the conviction that the social sciences could contribute more effectively than they have to managerial progress with respect to the human side of enterprise."[1]

He also emphasizes that managers themselves should be aware of advancements in knowledge about human behavior. As he puts it: "The professional need not be a scientist, but he must be sophisticated enough to make competent use of scientific knowledge."[2]

McGregor believed that employees naturally want to do good work. This motivation comes from taking pride in their accomplishments and satisfying their responsibilities. Based on research in the social sciences that has highlighted the human need for growth and learning, McGregor called for the development of a new management theory in which managers see their employees as human resources.

When managers acknowledge their employees' need for growth, McGregor showed, they also encourage learning, and participation with and for the organization as a whole. Unfortunately, at the time, employers did not see their employees in this way; as McGregor put it, "conventional managerial strategies for the organization, direction, and control of the human resources of enterprise are admirably suited to the capacities and characteristics of the child rather than the adult."[3]

McGregor expressed and defended his views so successfully that he soon became regarded as one of the most significant contributors to the field of organizational development* (an academic field of study focused on understanding and managing how large entities, like companies and corporations, change and evolve). *The Human Side of Enterprise* has been an important reference for generations of scholars, and today has been cited approximately 10,000 times.

> *"Behind every managerial decision or action are assumptions about human nature and human behavior."*
> —— Douglas McGregor, *The Human Side of Enterprise*

Author's Life

McGregor was born in 1906 in Detroit, Michigan. When he was young, he worked for the McGregor Institute,* a charitable organization founded by his grandfather in 1895. The Institute's mission was to help those who were struggling to find work or who could not sustain themselves on the work they could find. As well as providing food and shelter for around a thousand people each year, it offered direction and religious support. His work with the Institute helped McGregor become aware of the issues that working people faced.

McGregor attended City College of Detroit (now Wayne State University) and Oberlin College in Ohio. He then attended the prestigious psychology program at Harvard University, where in 1935 he earned his PhD. He worked at Harvard for two years before being hired by the Massachusetts Institute of Technology (MIT) as the first faculty member specializing in social psychology (the scientific study of the workings of the mind in a social context).[4]

In addition to his career at MIT, McGregor worked as a consultant with a rubber and sealants company. He helped negotiate contracts and train foremen; he also handled grievances and advised as to how the organization should be structured. This allowed him to test and apply his theories in the real world.

In 1948, McGregor became president of Antioch College, a progressive university in Yellow Springs, Ohio—one of the first mainstream colleges in the United States to accept African American students. Six years later, McGregor returned to MIT, where he became a faculty member of the Sloan School of Management.[5] It was during this time at MIT that McGregor helped found the academic field of organizational development in the late 1950s and early 1960s.[6] He died in 1964 of a heart attack, four years after the publication of *The Human Side of Enterprise.*

Author's Background

McGregor came of age in Detroit, a city that would become one of the nation's leading industrial centers and the automobile capital of the world.[7] During his childhood, the assembly line was invented and was put to use in factories. The assembly line had an enormous effect on businesses, as it allowed for the mass production of goods. It changed the very nature of work; instead of working on one car at a time, workers were assigned specialized tasks that affected a small part of a car's overall production.

McGregor's career was also shaped by the Great Depression* of the 1930s—a grave financial crisis that saw millions lose their jobs and face poverty. McGregor worked for his family's Institute during the early years of the Depression, helping to provide temporary accommodation for migrant workers.[8] McGregor would note later that while part-time workers and the unemployed struggled during the Depression, "Management was [also] subjected to severe pressures."[9]

McGregor had a close relationship with his father, who was also involved with the Institute. During his life, they exchanged letters in which they discussed their philosophies. Though they were both compassionate, McGregor believed more strongly than his father in people's innate goodness.

1. Douglas McGregor, *The Human Side of Enterprise* (New York: McGraw-Hill, 1960), 5.

2. McGregor, *The Human Side of Enterprise*, 5.

3. McGregor, *The Human Side of Enterprise*, 43.

4. MIT Sloan School of Management, "Pioneered at MIT Sloan," accessed November 19, 2015, http://mitsloan.mit.edu/faculty/spotlight/pioneered.php.

5. Managers-Net, "Douglas McGregor," accessed November 19, 2015, www.managers-net.com/Biography/mcgregor.html.

6. MIT Sloan, "Pioneered at MIT Sloan."

7. McGregor Fund, "History," accessed November 19, 2015, www.mcgregorfund.org/about-us/history.

8. Managers-Net, "Douglas McGregor."

9. McGregor, *The Human Side of Enterprise*, 46.

MODULE 2
ACADEMIC CONTEXT

KEY POINTS

* Traditionally, the primary method of industrial management was informed by the principles of scientific management,* an approach founded on the assumption that employees can be managed along scientific lines.
* The working conditions of any business are determined by managers' assumptions about human nature and what motivates employees.
* In 1954, a grant from the nonprofit Alfred P. Sloan Foundation,* which provides grants for education and research into science and technology, gave McGregor and his colleagues an opportunity to conduct systematic study into what makes a good manager.

The Work In its Context

Douglas McGregor's *The Human Side of Enterprise* responded to the existing consensus on management techniques. During the early twentieth century, managers exerted strict control over their employees, telling them what to do, and how and when to do it. Workers were rewarded or punished based on how well they performed in these circumstances; poor performance could result in a worker being fired.

Managers were often scrutinized by upper management; McGregor observed, for example, that many big corporations required managers to have annual physical examinations, and data based on these physicals were then used in decisions about that manager's future—whether or not he or she should be promoted, for example.[1] McGregor believed this showed that corporations exerted excessive control over both employees and managers.

As a consequence of these conditions, American society in the 1930s and 1940s was concerned with the ethics of managerial policies. Important regulations about child labor, employment of women, workers' compensation, and the right to collective bargaining (when laborers organize themselves to negotiate with their employers collectively) were being considered and passed. These restrictions obstructed a manager's freedom to exert control over employees, and were typically viewed by managers as unreasonable, but they ultimately improved working conditions. By the 1950s, workers enjoyed higher standards of living, and employers were paying more attention to what sorts of working conditions could improve employee job satisfaction.[2]

> *"Classical organization theory suffers from 'ethnocentrism': it ignores the significance of the political, social, and economic milieu in shaping organizations and influencing managerial practice."*
>
> —— Douglas McGregor, *The Human Side of Enterprise*

Overview of the Field

In the early twentieth century, management practices were rooted in the scientific management principles of Frederick Winslow Taylor,* a nineteenth-century engineer. Taylor's views on management, control, and the organization of work significantly influenced many corporations of his time.

An important aspect of Taylor's managerial theory is that workers should work faster and thereby generate greater output. Taylor studied factory workers, timing them with a stopwatch to see how long it took them to accomplish a particular task. He believed that the standard should be set by the worker whose productivity was fastest.

Holding workers to such standards became widely adopted, especially once technological innovations such as the assembly line were implemented and workers began to perform smaller, repetitive tasks. Taylor predicted that increasing worker productivity would lead to higher profits for the company, which in turn would lead to higher wages for employees.

Taylor's theory was based on his belief that people have a "natural instinct and tendency ... to take it easy, which may be called natural soldiering."[*3] Working slowly, he argued, causes fellow workers who would otherwise work hard to also work slowly—a concept Taylor called "systematic soldiering."[*] Systematic soldiering threatens an organization's profits, since it has a negative effect on production.

Academic Influences

McGregor's training in psychology inspired him to draw on fellow psychologists in exploring group dynamics[*] (the study of how people behave in groups), a field of study that dates as far back as the 1930s. One particularly important figure in group dynamics was Kurt Lewin,[*] a German American psychologist who studied leadership and how it influences group performance. According to the development consultant Anthony Lerner,* Lewin and his colleagues "were not guided merely by intellectual curiosity. They were guided by a sense of urgency to better understand aspects of group behavior that fostered democracy and individual choice in participation."[4]

McGregor was also influenced by the intellectual culture at MIT. In the early 1950s, during a meeting of the Advisory Committee of MIT's School of Industrial Management, the wealthy automotive business executive Alfred Sloan* posed questions about successful managers that encouraged McGregor to engage in systematic research into different management styles; in 1954, he received a grant from Sloan's nonprofit Sloan Foundation that enabled him to do so.

McGregor was also influenced by those he worked with, such as the management scholar Theodore M. Alfred,* who was one of his graduate students. Their joint study, in which they interviewed managers,[5] laid the groundwork for *The Human Side of Enterprise.* It is likely that McGregor also shared knowledge with Alex Bavelas,* an American psychologist and professor of business management, and another faculty member at MIT.

---

1. Douglas McGregor, *The Human Side of Enterprise* (New York: McGraw-Hill, 1960), 13.

2. McGregor, *The Human Side of Enterprise*, 12.

3. Frederick Winslow Taylor, "Fundamentals of Scientific Management," in *Working in America:*

Continuity, Conflict, and Change, ed. Amy S. Wharton (Mountain View, CA: Mayfield Publishing Company, 1998), 67–75.

4. Arthur Lerner, "McGregor's Legacy: Thoughts on What He Left, What Transpired, and What Remains to Pursue," *Journal of Management History* 17, no. 2 (2011): 219.

5. McGregor, *The Human Side of Enterprise*, v.

THE PROBLEM

KEY POINTS

* Managers' assumptions about human behavior decide how they treat their subordinates.

* Management styles of the early to mid-twentieth century were based on faulty understandings of human behavior.

* Traditional organizational theory reflected neither current understandings about technology nor social science research into human behavior.

Core Question

During a meeting of the Advisory Council of the School of Industrial Management at MIT, the businessman Alfred Sloan* articulated two questions that would become important for McGregor: What makes a successful manager? And are "successful managers born or made?"[1]

In 1954 a grant from the Sloan Foundation* (an organization founded to support research and education in innovative science and technology) allowed McGregor to pursue these questions by examining manager training programs in a variety of large companies to "learn more about the way in which theories and practices within different organizations influence the making of managers."[2] The study also tried to determine what kinds of people have the ability to become managers, as well as how employers can encourage their employees to learn and grow.

McGregor studied what managers actually did on a day-to-day

basis; he observed their interactions with both their own managers and their subordinates. He determined that managers' assumptions about human behavior greatly influenced their interactions with their subordinates. As a result, he conducted a systematic study of assumptions held by top managers about "the most effective way to manage people."[3]

McGregor's book therefore addresses four core questions:
- What makes a good manager?
- What are managers' assumptions about human nature?
- Are these assumptions correct or false?
- Are recent developments within the social sciences applied in organizations?

> "If there is a single assumption which pervades conventional organizational theory it is that authority is the central, indispensable means of managerial control. This is the basic principle of organization in the textbook theory of management. The very structure of the organization is a hierarchy of authoritative relationships."
>
> —— Douglas McGregor, *The Human Side of Enterprise*

The Participants

Douglas McGregor was a proponent of humanistic* management— a philosophy that values individual growth and learning. He was inspired by psychologists such as Kurt Lewin,* who explored group dynamics* in the 1930s. He also drew on other scholars, such as the social worker Mary Parker Follett,* who is seen as a pioneer in organizational behavior, the Australian psychologist Elton Mayo,* who specialized in group dynamics, and the psychologist Abraham Maslow,* who developed an important model of human behavior known as Maslow's hierarchy of needs.*[4]

McGregor learned from Mayo that workers value belonging to a group more than they value monetary rewards. Mayo also argued that worker satisfaction was dependent on cooperation and socialization within the working environment. That is, he claimed that workers who are socially satisfied are also more productive.[5]

McGregor's theoretical underpinning came from Abraham Maslow's *A Theory of Human Motivation*, which describes Maslow's hierarchy of needs and his concept of self-actualization* (a person's desire to develop his or her creative potential).[6] McGregor based his argument for the sort of perspective on human behavior that managers should have on Maslow's hierarchy.

In Maslow's hierarchy, human needs are broken down into different levels. At the bottom are physiological needs: the need for food and shelter. Next come safety needs: the need to live and work in a safe environment. These are followed by social needs: the need for meaningful relationships and meaningful work. Next are esteem needs: needs related to self-respect and self-confidence. And at the top of the hierarchy are self-actualization needs—those relating to reaching one's full creative potential.

While traditional management strategies only concerned themselves with physiological and safety needs, the bottom two levels, McGregor proposed that management should also aim to satisfy the higher-level needs, and that doing so would lead to higher job satisfaction and increased productivity.

The Contemporary Debate

At the beginning of the twentieth century, there was an important debate within the social sciences about the future of organizational theory. The classical theorists, who adopted the notion of Sigmund Freud* (often called the father of psychoanalysis*) that human beings are idle by nature and will not work hard unless controlled and incentivized,[7] were often at odds with those in the field of behavioral management,* initially developed by the American psychologists John B. Watson* and B. F. Skinner.*[8] Behavioral management theorists believed that management practices should account for the human need for growth and learning.

The postwar period*—a period of adjustment during which millions of soldiers returned home from fighting in World War II—allowed researchers to study how organizations structure themselves and manage their employees. During this time, McGregor and others who aligned themselves with behavioral management challenged the scientific management* theories that stipulated that workers need to be strictly controlled.

Behavioral management theorists like McGregor and management consultant Peter Drucker* applied humanistic values to management and organizational leadership. McGregor himself was able to use his training in psychology to critique classical management principles. He introduced important psychological concepts that applied human motivation and behavior to employee development, and also studied the extent to which knowledge derived from the social sciences could be implemented in various organizations.

1. Douglas McGregor, *The Human Side of Enterprise* (New York: McGraw-Hill, 1960), v.

2. McGregor, *The Human Side of Enterprise*, vi.

3. McGregor, *The Human Side of Enterprise*, vii.

4. Abraham Maslow, "A Theory of Human Motivation," *Psychological Review* 50 (1943): 370–96; Abraham Maslow, *Motivation and Personality* (New York: Harper & Row, 1954).

5. Managers-Net, "George Elton Mayo," accessed November 20, 2015, www. managers-net.com/ Biography/Mayo.html.

6. Maslow, "Human Motivation," 370–96.

7. Sigmund Freud, "An Outline of Psycho-analysis," *International Journal of Psychoanalysis* 21 (1940): 27–84.

8. John B. Watson, "Psychology as the Behaviorist Views It," *Psychological Review* 20 (1913): 158–77.

MODULE 4

THE AUTHOR'S CONTRIBUTION

KEY POINTS

* McGregor focused on a systematic analysis of contemporary management styles and their effectiveness within organizations.

* McGregor wanted to draw the attention of those working in management to new psychological understandings about human motivation.

* He believed that these new psychological understandings could form the basis for new management strategies and practices.

Author's Aims

Douglas McGregor, the author of *The Human Side of Enterprise*, spent his career trying to understand the complicated ways in which organizations work and are structured; he wanted to learn whether or not working conditions could be designed to accommodate both the company's objectives and their employees' personal needs. Previously, it had been thought that authority, hierarchy, and control were key to motivating people to work. Key principles developed by psychologists about human motivation, and seeing people as resources, had not yet been adopted.

McGregor wanted to demonstrate that these traditional management strategies were based on obsolete notions about human behavior, and that they hampered efficiency and productivity. Referring to these strategies, he wrote, "We will be unlikely to improve our managerial competence by blaming people for failing to behave according to our predictions."[1] That is, companies using traditional management practices should not blame their employees when those practices fail to produce results.

In addition to adopting principles from the field of psychology, McGregor also wanted to develop a management theory firmly rooted in humanism,* a philosophy that values individual human beings and their right to realize their full potential.

McGregor's theories helped modernize the way in which businesses structure themselves and view their employees. He helped promote the idea that taking a more humane view of workers not only improves their satisfaction, but also increases productivity.

> *"It will be clear to the reader that I believe many of our present assumptions about the most effective way to manage people are far from adequate."*
> —— Douglas McGregor, *The Human Side of Enterprise*

Approach

McGregor's approach included an analysis of management styles within organizations. He systematically studied prevailing assumptions about human behavior within the organizational context; specifically, he wanted to make the case that organizations whose view of human behavior was derived from the work of Sigmund Freud,* and from the "scientific" theories of the early management scholar Frederick Winslow Taylor,* do not offer their workers an environment conducive to effectiveness, efficiency, and productivity. Those organizations do not fully use the potential of their human resources.

McGregor was certain that psychological and social science research could contribute to more effective methods of management—methods that would benefit both employers *and* employees. He built on the work of the organizational theorist and industrial researcher Elton Mayo* and the psychologist Abraham Maslow* to show that working in groups makes people happier and more productive.

Throughout *The Human Side of Enterprise*, McGregor argues that managers should examine how their assumptions about human behavior affect the way they treat their subordinates. McGregor's insights helped organizations create more satisfying and efficient working conditions so that both they and their employees could thrive.

Contribution in Context

McGregor was among the first to express suspicion about how employees had traditionally been supervised, and to argue that management needed to adjust its view of human ability. Even after this view became popularized, however, McGregor's work stood out from that of his peers; he was able to combine important research from various fields and present it in a way that was easy to understand.

McGregor described two main theories of management, which he called Theory X* and Theory Y.* Theory X, the traditional theory, assumed that people were lazy and needed to be strictly controlled or rewarded depending on their performance.

According to Theory Y, people want to experience growth not only financially, but intellectually and emotionally. McGregor argued that modern businesses should shift away from Theory X practices, and proposed Theory Y as an alternative.

It was also important for McGregor that managers consider their own styles and beliefs about people before adopting a new approach. Theory X styles reflected a negative stance on human motivation. Managers who ascribed to these traditional practices did not account for self-initiative* (the ability of employees to begin projects without being told to do so by their managers) and trust in the workplace. As McGregor described it: "People, deprived of opportunities to satisfy at work the needs which are now important to them, behave exactly as we might predict— with indolence, passivity, unwillingness to accept responsibility, resistance to change ... [and] unreasonable demands for economic benefits. It would seem that we may be caught in a web of our own weaving."[2] Theory X management practices, he believed, led to poor productivity and unsatisfied workers.

McGregor's alternative approach to managing workers, Theory Y, attempted to account for Elton Mayo's discovery that people like working in groups, and for Abraham Maslow's hierarchy of needs,* a psychological model that described a range of motivations for human behavior. McGregor wrote that "Unless there are opportunities *at work* to satisfy these higher-level needs, people will be deprived; and their behavior will reflect this deprivation."[3]

To avoid feeling deprived, McGregor believed, employees

need to feel that their work is meaningful, and that they have the respect and fellowship of their colleagues. They also gain satisfaction from learning and collaborating.

Ultimately, McGregor provided an important insight into how enterprises could modernize working conditions, which was a central issue for those studying organizational development* (the study of how large entities such as businesses and institutions develop and evolve).

---

1. Douglas McGregor, *The Human Side of Enterprise* (New York: McGraw-Hill, 1960), 11.
2. McGregor, *The Human Side of Enterprise*, 42.
3. McGregor, *The Human Side of Enterprise*, 40.

SECTION 2
IDEAS

MODULE 5
MAIN IDEAS

KEY POINTS

- Classical organizational theory, which McGregor called Theory X,* is based on faulty assumptions about human behavior and motivation.
- The reward and punishment system of Theory X is counter-productive.
- McGregor's alternative, which he called Theory Y,* helps managers design working conditions that provide for employee self-esteem, status, and self-actualization.*

Key Themes

In *The Human Side of Enterprise*, Douglas McGregor distinguishes between two different management approaches, which he calls Theory X and Theory Y, showing how each shapes an organization's culture. He hopes to show by this comparison that Theory Y is better for both employees and employers; he also provides a theoretical explanation for how adopting the more humanistic* Theory Y will lead to better outcomes for businesses.

McGregor writes that Theory X is based on incentives: "The practical logic of incentives is that people want money, and that they will work harder to get more of it."[1] According to Theory X, then, people will accept strict controls as long as they are financially rewarded.

However, the book's key point is that this theory is based on a misunderstanding of human nature. The Theory X system fails to create productive, satisfying working conditions, because it does not account for a number of other important factors that influence human behavior, assuming instead that people are naturally lazy. As McGregor observes: "Theory X offers management an easy rationalization for ineffective organizational performance: It is due to the nature of the human resources with which we must work."[2]

> "We can improve our ability to control only if we recognize that control consists in selective adaptation to human nature rather than in attempting to make human nature conform to our wishes."
>
> —— Douglas McGregor, *The Human Side of Enterprise*

Exploring the Ideas

McGregor identified three main assumptions about human behavior as held by Theory X.

- "The average human being has an inherent dislike of work and will avoid it if he can."[3]
- "Because of this human characteristic of dislike of work, most people must be coerced, controlled, directed, threatened with punishment to get them to put forth adequate effort toward the achievement of organizational objectives."[4]
- "The average human being prefers to be directed, wishes to avoid responsibility, has relatively little ambition, [and] wants security above all."[5]

If people will only work when coerced and controlled, then they can be managed through a system of rewards and punishments.

McGregor calls such a system "the carrot-and-stick motivation" of employees. Under Theory X, employees will only perform work for incentives such as money (the "carrot") and to avoid being disciplined or even fired (the "stick").

The carrot-and-stick system works reasonably well when people are struggling to pay for basic necessities like food and shelter. And indeed, McGregor notes that management can control employees by providing or withholding these needs: "Man tends to live for bread alone when there is little bread."[6]

Additionally, McGregor argues that work itself should be a motivating experience. If the only benefit of work is the creation of wages to be spent outside work, then work begins to look like a form of punishment: something employees only do to make the rest of their lives satisfying. This is problematic, because, as McGregor puts it, companies could "hardly expect them to undergo more of this punishment than is necessary."[7]

For this reason, McGregor believes that work itself should be a satisfying experience: it should bring meaning and self-respect. He proposes an alternative to Theory X that would meet these other, "higher-order," needs. He calls it Theory Y, and its basic assumptions are rooted in the psychological research of the psychologists Abraham Maslow* and Elton Mayo.*

Theory Y's main assumptions are that:
- "[People] will exercise self-direction and self-control in the service of objectives to which [they are] committed."[8]
- "The average human being learns, under proper conditions, not only to accept but to seek responsibility."[9]

- "The capacity to exercise a relatively high degree of imagination, ingenuity, and creativity in the solution of organizational problems is widely, not narrowly, distributed in the population."[10]
- "Under the conditions of modern industrial life, the intellectual potentialities of the average human being are only partially utilized."[11]

Theory Y assumes that employees can grow and develop in the workplace, and that management should explore the potential of human resources, and selectively adapt strategies to individual employees. In addition to the inherent reward of learning new skills at work, Theory Y suggests that employees have needs "that relate to [their] reputation[s]: needs for status, for recognition, for appreciation, for the deserved respect of one's fellows."[12] In this way, Theory Y tries to bring management practices up to date via contemporary notions of human behavior.

Language and Expression

McGregor wanted his theories to make a difference in both the scholarly field of management science, and the real world of management. As such, *The Human Side of Enterprise* was written to inspire both scholars and people in the business community.[13] McGregor was able to draw on his experience as a consultant at a rubber and sealants company to reach an audience outside academia.

McGregor came to be regarded as one of the most significant contributors to the field of organizational development.* Because he wanted his book to be accessible to managers, he included a few chapters that function as a guide to implementing Theory Y in any business enterprise. As a consequence, *The Human Side of Enterprise* has had a massive impact on both business scholars and the business community itself.

1. Douglas McGregor, *The Human Side of Enterprise* (New York: McGraw-Hill, 1960*)*, 9.

2. McGregor, *The Human Side of Enterprise*, 48.

3. McGregor, *The Human Side of Enterprise*, 33.

4. McGregor, *The Human Side of Enterprise*, 34.

5. McGregor, *The Human Side of Enterprise*, 34.

6. McGregor, *The Human Side of Enterprise*, 41.

7. McGregor, *The Human Side of Enterprise*, 40.

8. McGregor, *The Human Side of Enterprise*, 47.

9. McGregor, *The Human Side of Enterprise*, 48.

10. McGregor, *The Human Side of Enterprise*, 48.

11. McGregor, *The Human Side of Enterprise*, 48.

12. McGregor, *The Human Side of Enterprise*, 38.

13. Peter Vaill, "Process Wisdom for a New Age," *ReVISION* 7, no. 2 (1986): 39–49.

MODULE 6
SECONDARY IDEAS

KEY POINTS

* One challenge for McGregor's Theory Y* is that it is difficult to evaluate worker performance: when employees direct themselves, how should wages and salary raises be determined?

* McGregor recommended using the Scanlon Plan,* which was invented by steelworker and local union president Joseph Scanlon* during the 1930s. The Scanlon Plan was based on employee participation and cost-reduction sharing* (in which employees receive a share of the company's profits).

* Theory Y's objectives for managers have not been widely implemented today because companies have not devoted themselves to promoting learning and growth among their workers.

Other Ideas

An important secondary idea in *The Human Side of Enterprise* is Douglas McGregor's exploration of how performance reviews might be changed to reflect the assumptions of Theory Y. According to one scholarly analysis, performance reviews during McGregor's time "were mostly performed in a manner consistent with Theory X. That is, they were unilateral in nature and clearly represented a method of external control by the supervisor, manager and the organization."[1] McGregor suggested that changing how workers were evaluated could positively reshape an entire organization.

McGregor introduced a method of appraisal characterized by a dialogue between different organizational levels, notably between lower and high-ranking managers and their employees, for the purpose of nurturing cooperation. McGregor advocated synchronizing employees' goals with those of the company; he argued that performance reviews should not result in reward or punishment, but, rather, should encourage employees at all levels to participate in improving the company's performance.

> "A still greater degree of participation would be involved if the superior were to present his subordinates a problem facing him with the request that they help him find the best solution to it."
>
> ——Douglas McGregor, *The Human Side of Enterprise*

Exploring the Ideas

McGregor argued that employees should have more control over their tasks and responsibilities, and that those responsibilities should be aligned with the organization's overall objectives. This method of management was first introduced by management consultant Peter Drucker* in his *The Practice of Management* (1954) and is now commonly known as "management by objectives (MBO)."*

McGregor builds on Drucker's method by focusing on how relationships can be built within an organization. Performance reviews, he believed, should be based on the results of those relationships, and not on an individual's performance alone.[2] This creates an organizational structure that is humanistic,* in that it values the growth and development of individual workers, and also one that draws on the knowledge of those who study behavioral management.

McGregor was also an advocate of the Scanlon Plan, named after the steelworker and unionist Joseph Scanlon (a union is an organization of workers founded to secure better working conditions or pay). The Scanlon Plan is a management philosophy that focuses on cost-reduction sharing and effective participation, consistent with Theory Y principles.[3]

Cost-reduction sharing means, according to McGregor, that employees share in the economic gains "from improvements in organizational performance."[4] They receive a monthly bonus on top of their wages depending on the output of the organization as a whole. This helps them "see the connection between their behavior and organizational achievement"—that is, it allows them to see their personal success as being tied up with the company's overall success.[5]

The other aspect of the Scanlon Plan—effective participation— means establishing committees in which employees meet for brief brainstorming sessions (that is, spontaneously developing, and then discussing, ideas). McGregor notes that, by doing this, the company receives "economically significant ideas" that could save them using the services of an outside consultant. These two principles—cost reduction sharing and effective participation—can also improve relationships between workers on the shop floor (the physical space where employees work).

Overlooked

Since its publication in 1960, *The Human Side of Enterprise* has been thoroughly examined by generations of academics. Businesses, however, have yet to truly adopt management models that promote employee self-actualization*—workers' opportunity to realize their full creative potential.

McGregor argued that if businesses were to promote self-actualization and humanistic values, they would benefit from increased worker satisfaction, which would in turn lead to better results (in terms of efficiency and productivity). It would also lead to a lower job turnover rate, and so reduce the costs of hiring and training new employees. In terms of the culture of the workplace and assumptions regarding the needs of employees, McGregor believed that Theory Y would work as a self-fulfilling prophecy were it to be fully adopted.[6]

Today, however, organizations fall short of "providing opportunities for self-actualization."[7] One reason for this is that employees now tend to change jobs at a much higher rate than when McGregor wrote *The Human Side of Enterprise*; as a result, organizations have come to reconsider how much to invest in employee development—including opportunities for self-actualization.[8]

1. Peter Sorensen and Matt Minahan, "McGregor's Legacy: The Evolution and Current Application of Theory Y Management," *Journal of Management History* 17, no. 2 (2011): 178–92.

2. Richard Babcock, "Tracing the History of MBO," in *Strategies and Tactics in Management by Objectives*, ed. Richard Babcock and Peter F. Sorensen (Champaign, IL: Stipes, 1976), 2–24.

3. Business Dictionary, "Scanlon Plan," accessed November 20, 2015, www.businessdictionary.com/

definition/scanlon-plan.html.

4. Douglas McGregor, *The Human Side of Enterprise* (New York; McGraw-Hill, 1960), 111.

5. McGregor, *The Human Side of Enterprise*, 112.

6. Sorensen and Minahan, "McGregor's Legacy."

7. Thomas C. Head, "Douglas McGregor's Legacy: Lessons Learned, Lessons Lost," *Journal of Management History* 17, no. 2 (2011): 202–16.

8. Rensis Likert, *The Human Organization: Its Management and Value* (New York: McGraw-Hill, 1967).

ACHIEVEMENT

KEY POINTS

* *The Human Side of Enterprise* began as an article of the same title.[1]
* McGregor cautioned that an environment dominated by Theory X* practices, founded on the assumptions that workers are idle and will operate only under strict control or for monetary incentives, is not conducive to the implementation of Theory Y* practices.
* McGregor acknowledged that applying Theory Y would take time, since many organizations had a long history of using Theory X management strategies.

Assessing the Argument

Although Douglas McGregor's *The Human Side of Enterprise* focuses on the controlling style of Theory X management—in particular, coercion and punishment—he also acknowledges that certain Theory X approaches are more subtle than others. Some managers are permissive, for example, focusing on satisfying employees' demands to achieve harmony in the workplace. Ultimately, McGregor notes, this subtler approach is simply another form of control and just as counterproductive as sterner strategies; it means that employees can expect more and give less effort in return.

McGregor claims that it does not matter what kind of Theory X management style is used, as all lead to the company failing to meet its economic objectives. Theory X practices also fail to create working conditions in which people thrive, since they meet only physiological needs (needs related to food and shelter) and safety needs (the desire to work in environments that are not dangerous).

On the other hand, under Theory Y strategy, management can be flexible enough to address its workforce's social needs (needs related to collaboration and sense of belonging) and egoistic needs (which include self-confidence, independence, achievement, knowledge, appreciation, status, and recognition). After that, organizations can work to fulfill their employees' self-actualization* needs.[2]

For McGregor, it was more important that management abandon its limiting assumptions about people, such as those identified in his Theory X, than that they accept the assumptions of Theory Y.[3] He did, however, hope that managers would develop their practices to account for the varied needs of their workers. So Theory Y was important insofar as it was a proposed replacement for Theory X, but McGregor did not see it as the only way forward.

> *"We tend to think that the boss is a boss. This is not the case at all. The circumstances change from hour to hour, and from day to day as the manager undertakes different activities, and the methods of influence which are appropriate shift accordingly."*
>
> —— Douglas McGregor, *The Human Side of Enterprise*

Achievement in Context

McGregor first presented his theory that classical management theories were based on false assumptions about human behavior to the very managers he was studying, and was glad to learn that "an increasing number of managers recognize the inadequacy of present methods."[4] He then shared the research with his colleagues at the School of Industrial Management at MIT.

In this way, McGregor was able to receive feedback about his ideas from both his research subjects and his colleagues; the feedback informed an article, also titled "The Human Side of Enterprise," which he published in 1957. His Theories X and Y sparked a dialogue within the community of management scholars that encouraged him to refine his ideas, eventually presenting them in their most fully developed forms in *The Human Side of Enterprise.*

When his work was first published, managers were receptive to a shift from Theory X to Theory Y objectives. McGregor's argument that businesses would be unable to increase their productivity and efficiency unless they could satisfy workers' needs, as described in Maslow's hierarchy,* was made successfully.

McGregor's Theory X and Theory Y led to substantial research on psychology and management within the field of organizational development.* Moreover, his ideas have been adopted by and have influenced a number of other academic disciplines, among them organizational behavior, leadership, strategy, and human resource management (the management of workers, skills, employment policy, and so on).

Limitations

McGregor himself was the first to acknowledge the limitations of Theory Y, writing: "Theoretical assumptions such as those of Theory Y imply some conditions which are unrealizable in practice."[5] He did not see this as a "handicap," however, but as a "stimulus to invention and discovery."[6]

McGregor also realized that some organizations would find it easier to adopt the assumptions of Theory Y than others. It is difficult, if not impossible, for organizations with a long history of Theory X practices to make the transition: major changes in management styles require a complete overhaul in terms of structure, functions, and the sort of people employed as managers.

That said, McGregor does offer a detailed account of how businesses might adopt Theory Y within a short amount of time. He provides an in-depth analysis of organizational theories in order to spark discussion among scholars and the business community; his work advocates collaboration in the area of human resources in industry.[7]

---

1. Douglas McGregor, "The Human Side of Enterprise," first published in *Adventure in Thought and Action*, Proceedings of the Fifth Anniversary Convocation of the School of Industrial Management, Massachusetts Institute of Technology, Cambridge, April 9, 1957 (Cambridge, MA: MIT School of Industrial Management, 1957); reprinted in *The Management Review* 46 (1957): 22–8.

2. Douglas McGregor, *The Human Side of Enterprise* (New York: McGraw-Hill, 1960), 38.

3. McGregor, *The Human Side of Enterprise*, 245.

4. McGregor, *The Human Side of Enterprise*, 245.

5. McGregor, *The Human Side of Enterprise*, 245.

6. McGregor, *The Human Side of Enterprise*, 246.

7. McGregor, *The Human Side of Enterprise*, 246.

PLACE IN THE AUTHOR'S WORK

KEY POINTS

- McGregor devoted his career to analyzing the relationship between management styles and worker efficiency. *The Human Side of Enterprise* was his most influential academic work.
- He linked Theory X* practices to a lack of innovation and efficiency.
- McGregor's publications were significant throughout the twentieth century.

Positioning

Douglas McGregor's *The Human Side of Enterprise* offers the insights gleaned from a career spent analyzing management styles; he focused on the importance of staff-line* relationships (the relationships between managers and those they manage) as having the greatest influence on working conditions. McGregor was a staunch humanist,* and believed that workers should be valued as people and given the opportunity to grow.

According to the organizational theorists Daniel Katz* and Robert Kahn,* McGregor's Theory Y* uses "referent power"*—influence based on liking or identification with another person.[1] McGregor advocated collaboration and participation between employees and managers, believing this would strengthen their relationships; Katz and Kahn believed that organizations would be more effective if all their members were able to collaborate and participate with their coworkers.[2]

McGregor touted Theory Y as the management style that would generate the greatest employee satisfaction and the highest productivity. According to Peter Senge,* a management theorist and senior lecturer at MIT, McGregor shows why it is difficult for companies governed by Theory X to innovate—but Theory Y does not necessarily guarantee innovation either.[3]

Unfortunately, McGregor did not have the opportunity to address concerns such as those of Senge; he died only four years after *The Human Side of Enterprise* was published.

> *"The purpose of this volume is not to entice management to choose sides over Theory X or Theory Y. It is, rather, to encourage the realization that theory is important, to urge management to examine its assumptions and make them explicit. In doing so, it will open a door to the future."*
>
> ——Douglas McGregor, *The Human Side of Enterprise*

Integration

While criticizing management under Theory X, McGregor pointed out that contemporary management practices had "significantly reduced economic hardships, eliminated the more extreme forms of industrial warfare, provided a generally safe and pleasant working environment, but it has done all these things without changing its fundamental theory of management."[4] That is: while Theory X management had satisfied basic needs, it had not gone far enough to change working conditions. Productivity could still improve if organizations changed their assumptions about how employees should be treated.

But not everyone agreed with McGregor's assessment. His claims were based on the psychological dynamics that occur in relationships between managers and their subordinates. Critics therefore argued that McGregor did not account for environmental factors such as the culture in which the business was located, or the economic and legal consequences of government regulation. They argued that these could also affect organizations and reduce efficiency.[5]

A number of companies also rejected McGregor's suggestion that high-ranked officials carried the greatest responsibility for stagnant productivity.

Significance

McGregor anticipated the intellectual needs and movements of his time. When his theories were introduced, they helped modernize the ways in which businesses were structured and managed. His work is important because it combines psychological and managerial concepts, and, in so doing, encourages managers to self-reflect, and to see their workers more humanistically.

In general, McGregor's work has been positively received in organizational management, and he is often referenced in management textbooks. In fact, according to a poll conducted by the *Economist* in 1993, McGregor is the most popular management scholar of all time.[6]

The Human Side of Enterprise itself has also been popular, having been voted the fourth most significant management text of the twentieth century by the Academy of Management, publisher of the highly respected *Academy of Management Journal*. The book was listed in the "25 Most Influential Business Management Books" by *Time* magazine in 2011.[7]

---

1. Daniel Katz and Robert L. Kahn, *The Social Psychology of Organizations* (New York: John Wiley & Sons, 1966), 302.

2. Katz and Kahn, *Social Psychology of Organizations*, 303.

3. Peter M. Senge, "The Practice of Innovation," *Leader to Leader* 9 (1998): 16–22.

4. Douglas McGregor, *The Human Side of Enterprise* (New York: McGraw-Hill, 1960), 46.

5. Warren Bennis, "Chairman Mac in Perspective," *Journal of Management History* 17, no. 2 (2011): 1–11.

6. Tim Hindle, *Guide to Management Ideas and Gurus* (London: Profile Books, 2008).

7. "The 25 Most Influential Business Management Books," *Time*, accessed November 20, 2015, http://content.time.com/time/specials/packages/completelist/0,29569,2086680,00.html.

SECTION 3
IMPACT

THE FIRST RESPONSES

KEY POINTS

* *The Human Side of Enterprise* attracted a great deal of scholarly attention when it was first published in 1960.

* McGregor was criticized by those who favored traditional management styles.

* Some argued that McGregor's Theory Y* misrepresented human nature.

Criticism

Douglas McGregor's critique of Theory X* in *The Human Side of Enterprise* was itself criticized by those who favored traditional management techniques. They accused McGregor of having a "distorted" idea of human nature.[1] In particular, they believed that human beings behave differently in different settings; workplace behavior is not the same as family or community behavior.

Additionally, McGregor's humanistic* values provoked criticism, even though his tone had been moderate and objective. And while the influential psychologist Abraham Maslow's* hierarchy of needs* provided a firm foundation for Theory Y, the theory had its limits—which meant that McGregor's work likewise had limits. In fact, Maslow himself was one of McGregor's critics; he believed that Theory Y was too idealistic and impractical to apply to workplaces.[2]

Other critics, such as McGregor's colleague at MIT, Edgar Schein,* agreed with Maslow;[3] for Schein, while Theory Y's assumptions about human nature are realistic, management does not have a responsibility to include employees in the decision-making process.[4] As such, he believed that Theory Y should only be applied to those in upper management positions.[5]

McGregor was also criticized for the way he obtained and interpreted data. One scholar observed: "McGregor based his arguments in part on impressionistic observation and practiced hypothesis testing only in a casual manner."[6] In other words, McGregor was so focused on improving employees' working conditions that he may have overlooked some of the challenges of implementing Theory Y.

> "... authority is an inappropriate method of control on which to place exclusive reliance in United States industry today ... under certain circumstances it may be essential, but for promoting collaboration it is at best a weak crutch."
> —— Douglas McGregor, *The Human Side of Enterprise*

Responses

Other responses were more nuanced. For example, Geert Hofstede,* the prominent Dutch cross-cultural psychologist* (a psychologist who examines psychological differences and similarities across cultural borders) suggested that both Theory X and Theory Y were based on overly broad assumptions about human nature. In particular, Hofstede argued that they do not take into account how uncertainty avoidance*—the degree to which people are willing to accept the unexpected—varies from culture to culture.

According to Hofstede, there are some countries in which people are less prepared to cope with uncertainty and should therefore have less influence on decision-making. In those situations, Theory X might work better than Theory Y. In the light of this, it seems unreasonable to advocate a total abandonment of Theory X practices.[7]

McGregor's work also served as a foundation for other academics, such as the management scholar William Ouchi,* who proposed Theory Z* in 1981.[8] Ouchi wanted to provide American companies with a competitive edge by implementing some of the characteristics of Japanese business corporations, which had been highly successful in the 1970s. At that time, Japanese companies provided lifelong employment and focused on employee well-being. This led to high employee morale and economic success.[9]

Conflict and Consensus

Among the challenges to his work, McGregor was particularly compelled to respond to Hofstede's critique that the culture in which an organization exists affects the effectiveness of Theory X or Theory Y. Hofstede urged McGregor to provide more details about which environments his theories were most applicable to.[10]

McGregor's colleague Edgar Schein initially defended McGregor by noting that Theory X and Theory Y are simply labels that describe two different sets of beliefs that managers seem to hold about their workers. McGregor did not demand that all organizations adopt Theory Y practices—he merely proposed Theory Y as a possible alternative to Theory X. In the introduction to McGregor's 1967 *The Professional Manager* (published after his death), Schein wrote that "few readers were willing to acknowledge that the content of Doug's book made such a neutral point."[11]

Those who later used McGregor's work were careful to adjust his ideas to account for the way in which culture influences work environments.

1. Harold Guetzkow, review of *Leadership and Organization: A Behavioral Science Approach* by Robert Tannenbaum, Irving R. Weschler, and Fred Massarik, *American Sociological Review* 26, no. 5 (1961): 804.

2. Abraham H. Maslow, *Eupsychian Management: A Journal* (Homewood, IL: Irwin, 1965).

3. Edgar Schein, "In Defense of Theory Y," *Organizational Dynamics* 4 (1975): 17–30.

4. Edgar Schein, "Relationships between Sex Role Stereotypes and Requisite Management Characteristics among Female Managers," *Journal of Applied Psychology* 60, no. 3 (1975): 340–4.

5. David Jacobs, "Book Review Essay: Douglas McGregor: The Human Side of Enterprise in Peril," *Academy of Management Review* 29, no. 2 (2004): 293–6.

6. Jacobs, "Book Review," 294.

7. Carol M. Sanchez and Dawn M. Curtis, "Different Minds and Common Problems: Geert Hofstede's Research on National Cultures," *Performance Improvement Quarterly* 13, no. 2 (2000): 9–19.

8. William G. Ouchi, *Theory Z: How American Business Can Meet the Japanese Challenge* (Reading, MA: Addison-Wesley, 1981).

9. Mind Tools Editorial Team, "Theory Z: Merging Eastern and Western Management Styles," accessed November 24, 2015, www.mindtools. com/pages/article/theory-z.htm.

10. Warren Bennis, "Chairman Mac in Perspective," *Journal of Management History* 17, no. 2 (2011): 1–11.

11. Douglas McGregor, *The Professional Manager* (New York: McGraw-Hill, 1967), 11.

MODULE 10
THE EVOLVING DEBATE

KEY POINTS

- McGregor successfully convinced many managers to adopt Theory Y* principles.

- Some of McGregor's ideas were used in combination with contingency theories* (theories about how management and leadership practices should adapt or change to match a market or culture).

- Those who built on McGregor's work identified specific circumstances and cultural contexts in which either Theory X* or Theory Y would be more applicable.

Uses and Problems

Douglas McGregor's theories, as discussed in his *The Human Side of Enterprise*, were speedily introduced into companies because they promised growth and increased efficiency. At the multinational consumer goods company Proctor and Gamble, for example, executives applied Theory Y to one of their manufacturing plants. They attempted to implement a management structure in which employees all held similar ranks, decision-making was determined by management by objectives ("MBO,"* according to which employees developed detailed plans to achieve company goals),[1] and in which performance was regularly monitored.[2] Ultimately, the plant increased its productivity by 30 percent.[3]

Managers generally accepted McGregor's proposal that applying Abraham Maslow's* hierarchy of needs* to the workplace would both improve employee collaboration and communication, and motivate workers to grow and learn. McGregor was not quite as successful within the scholarly community following the psychologist Geert Hofstede's* criticism that the success of Theory X or Theory Y depends on cultural context. That said, scholars still built upon the theories and ideas presented in *The Human Side of Enterprise*.

> "At times he [the manager] may be in the role of the leader of a group of subordinates; at other times he may be a member of a group of his peers. Sometimes he is in the role of teacher; at other times he may be a decision maker, a disciplinarian, a helper, a consultant, or simply an observer."
> —— Douglas McGregor, *The Human Side of Enterprise*

Schools of Thought

Scholars further explored the ways in which the implementation of Theories X and Y affect how organizations adapt and learn. For example, based on McGregor's work, the management theorist Peter Senge* coined the term "learning organization,"* which refers to companies that are able to transform themselves by encouraging their employees to learn.

Learning organizations are based on the idea that there is no best way to manage; instead, the best managers are able to adapt to new situations and to account for changing market environments. In other words, a strategy effective in one situation may be ineffective in another. This is also sometimes called contingency theory; today, a great deal of evidence exists to support it.[4]

In Current Scholarship

Today, scholars who draw on *The Human Side of Enterprise* take into account Hofstede's warnings about how Theories X and Y are affected by culture. This has opened new directions for research.

For example, the British professor of organization sociology Joan Woodward* argues that while Theory X is applicable to enterprises engaged in mass production, Theory Y is more relevant to those making complex, advanced products.[5] Edgar Schein,* McGregor's colleague at MIT, proposed a new version of Theory Y that was based not on humanistic* principles, but on those of contingency theory.[6]

Other scholars have argued that Theory X works in stable environments, and Theory Y in rapidly changing environments.[7] Still others suggest that various theories can be used in different departments of the same organization: managers can create varied working conditions depending on their beliefs and the culture of the department itself.[8]

Generally speaking, scholars have shifted their attention away from classifying management styles as X or Y, and from promoting humanistic values within organizations.[9]

---

1. Richard Babcock, "Tracing the History of MBO," in *Strategies and Tactics in Management by Objectives*, ed. Richard Babcock and Peter F. Sorensen (Champaign, IL: Stipes, 1976): 2–24.

2. "Management by Objectives," *Economist*, accessed November 20, 2015, www.economist.com/node/14299761.

3. Robert Waterman, *The Frontiers of Excellence: Learning from Companies That Put People First* (London: Nicholas Brealey Publishing, 1994).

4. David Jacobs, "Book Review Essay: Douglas McGregor: The Human Side of Enterprise in Peril," *Academy of Management Review* 29, no. 2 (2004): 293–6.

5. Joan Woodward, *Industrial Organization: Theory and Practice* (New York: Oxford University Press, 1965).

6. Edgar Schein, "Relationships between Sex Role Stereotypes and Requisite Management Characteristics among Female Managers," *Journal of Applied Psychology* 60, no. 3 (1975): 340–4.

7. Tom Burns and George M. Stalker, *The Management of Innovations* (London: Tavistock, 1961).

8. Paul R. Lawrence and Jay William Lorsch, "High Performing Organizations in Three Environments," in *Organization and Environment: Managing Differentiation and Integration*, ed. Paul R. Lawrence and Jay William Lorsch (Boston, MA: Harvard Business School, 1967), 133–58.

9. Don Hellriegel, Susan E. Jackson, and John W. Slocum, *Management: A Competency-Based Approach* (Cincinnati, OH: South-Western Publishing, 2002).

IMPACT AND INFLUENCE TODAY

KEY POINTS

* McGregor wanted to change how employees were evaluated.

* Scholars advocate that organizations become "learning organizations,"* defined by their ability to adapt to changing circumstances.

* McGregor continues to influence the conversation within the academic field of management.

Position

In *The Human Side of Enterprise*, Douglas McGregor linked a company's ability to innovate with its managers' ability to assess their own management styles, believing it important that they reflect on the ways in which their specific styles affect their employees.

Similarly, he argued that employees should be provided with objective feedback, and that managers should not conduct annual performance reviews. The problem with such reviews, he wrote, was that they "provided 'feedback' about behavior at a time remote from the behavior itself."[1] He also believed that individuals should not receive merit pay, since it is based on a manager's subjective opinion.

Instead, McGregor proposed group rewards that were based on objective measures of the group's performance. The most outstanding performers within a group would also be given a substantial bonus. However, individual merit pay, and not group pay, is still commonly awarded in American businesses.

A number of scholars continue to develop McGregor's work today. The management scholar Peter Senge* has elaborated on McGregor's ideas as to why it is important for managers to reflect on how their practices affect staff-line (or manager-subordinate) relationships.*[2] He has suggested that it is difficult for managers to notice their own assumptions about people if they are constantly focused on achieving goals.[3] And the American business theorist Chris Argyris* suggested that organizations that aspire to be learning organizations should create working conditions that encourage innovation, creativity, and efficiency.[4]

> "With every passing year, McGregor's message becomes ever more relevant, timelier and more important."
>
> —— Peter Drucker, in Sultan Kermally's
> *Gurus on People Management*

Interaction

Organizational behaviorists*—those who investigate the workings of organizations, on the basis that behavior offers important insight into human psychology—have supported McGregor's view that intense control mechanisms can cause employees to become submissive, and that this is ultimately bad for companies. An organization's leadership should use its power to create mutually beneficial relationships between managers and employees.

Following Geert Hofstede's* criticism that McGregor's Theory Y* does not account for cultural differences, scholars have erased the strict borders between Theories X* and Y. This means that discussions between proponents of each school have shifted away from defining types of management in these terms. Instead, newer "contingency theories"* combine elements of both. In this way, today's theories of management still incorporate McGregor's work.

One scholar recently acknowledged the value of *The Human Side of Enterprise* for the field of organizational management,* but also criticized it for focusing so much on the psychological relationship between managers and their employees, and perhaps for overlooking the culture of the entire organization.[5]

The Continuing Debate

Nearly five decades after McGregor published *The Human Side of Enterprise*, his work continues to influence scholarly literature about organizational development.*[6] His influence on the field is most obvious when we examine how often he is referred to in the work of other scholars.

McGregor was integral to scholarship throughout the 1980s. In 2000, *Douglas McGregor, Revisited: Managing the Human Side of the Enterprise* sparked new interest in his scholarship. The book contains excerpts of his work and is optimistic that, in the future, we can live in "a world of work that we could call 'McGregorian.'"[7]

In 2004, McGregor was praised for encouraging increased employee participation in the workplace. As one reviewer put it, "McGregor's moral outlook ... reflects [his] awareness of the consequences of management choice for workers."[8] In 2011, the

Journal of Management History devoted an entire issue, with contributions from different academics, to McGregor's legacy, contributions, and limitations.[9] A well-known management scholar wrote that McGregor has left "a lasting impression" on the world of business and management studies.[10]

It is clear, then, that McGregor's work remains relevant to today's discussion.

---

1. Douglas McGregor, *The Human Side of Enterprise* (New York: McGraw-Hill, 1960), 87.

2. Peter Senge, "The Practice of Innovation," *Leader to Leader* 9 (1998): 16–22.

3. Peter Senge, *The Fifth Discipline: The Art and Practice of the Learning Organization* (New York: Doubleday, 1990).

4. Chris Argyris, *Teaching Smart People How to Learn* (Boston, MA: Harvard Business Press, 1998).

5. Warren Bennis, "Chairman Mac in Perspective," *Journal of Management History* 17, no. 2 (2011): 1–11.

6. W. Warren Burke, *Organization Change: Theory and Practice* (Thousand Oaks, CA: Sage, 2008); W. Warren Burke, "The Douglas McGregor Legacy," *Journal of Applied Behavioral Science* 45 (2009): 8–11.

7. Gary Heil, Warren Bennis, and Deborah C. Stephens, *Douglas McGregor, Revisited: Managing the Human Side of the Enterprise* (New York: Wiley, 2000), viii.

8. David Jacobs, "Book Review Essay: Douglas McGregor: The Human Side of Enterprise in Peril," *Academy of Management Review* 29, no. 2 (2004): 293–6.

9. Peter F. Sorensen and Matt Minahan, "McGregor's Legacy: The Evolution and Current Application of Theory Y Management," *Journal of Management History* 17, no. 2 (2011): 178–92.

10. Robert A. Cunningham, "Douglas McGregor: A Lasting Impression," *Ivey Business Journal* 75 (2011): 5–7.

MODULE 12
WHERE NEXT?

KEY POINTS

* One reason McGregor's Theory Y* has not been widely implemented today is that companies tend to engage in short-term planning, which inhibits them from investing in employees' long-term growth.

* McGregor's *The Human Side of Enterprise* is valuable when interpreting current economic trends, such as the recent recession in the United States.

* Management under Theory X* may lead to offices that resemble "electronic sweatshops."*

Potential

As much as Douglas McGregor's *The Human Side of Enterprise* encouraged companies to invest in their employees' personal growth, today most companies engage in strategic planning that covers no more than the next three years of business.[1] This has created instability in the employment market, since companies do not plan for their employees' long-term futures; it also encourages human resource managers to hire employees who are already trained, rather than to spend time developing an untrained employee.[2]

One reason for this is that it is costly to invest in workers at a time when so many people change jobs frequently; these costs tend to offset the higher productivity that McGregor argued would result from Theory Y practices. That said, managers continue to draw on

Theory Y assumptions to encourage creativity and innovation.

The criticism that McGregor's work did not account for cultural differences is also still valid today. Twenty-first century companies have diverse workforces: their employees and managers come from a wide range of places and cultures. This means that organizations may differ from department to department, and varying styles of management may be effective for different employees.

It is exactly this aspect of McGregor's work that would benefit from further development. Adapting his theories for a multicultural context would update them for businesses today.

> *"... his moral perspective on human relations remains valuable even in altered circumstances. In fact, in this era of downsizing, pension insecurity, and aggressive investors seeking immediate return, it is useful to reconsider McGregor's call to honor the unfulfilled potential of employees."*
>
> —— David Jacobs, *Book Review Essay: Douglas McGregor: The Human Side of Enterprise in Peril*

Future Directions

The recent economic recession in the United States, dubbed the "Great Recession,"* illustrates the significance of McGregor's work. This period of economic downturn (2007–9) was characterized by higher unemployment (from 5 percent in 2007 to 10 percent in 2009), low wages, temporary employment, and deteriorating working conditions, including the loss of fringe benefits such as health insurance.[3] Millions of Americans struggled to find jobs that would pay the bills and provide for their families. This brings to mind McGregor's observation that "the individual can be controlled so long as he is struggling for subsistence. Man tends to live for bread alone when there is little bread."[4] High unemployment provided management with an opportunity to focus on economic objectives, and in the process to ignore workers' job satisfaction.

As a result, many companies today follow Theory X assumptions and principles; furthermore, they can now use technology that fits a Theory X approach, such as computer surveillance that allows them to monitor employees at all times. In modern call centers, for example, pop-ups may appear on employees' computer screens telling them they need to work faster. This has led some scholars to argue that these technologies transform offices into "electronic sweatshops."[5]

Summary

In *The Human Side of Enterprise,* Douglas McGregor contrasts two opposing types of management. Under Theory X, managers assume that employees want to do as little work as possible, and that a system of strict control and rewards is needed. In contrast, Theory Y management recognizes that employees need growth, learning, responsibility, and creativity to be good workers. McGregor is in favor of Theory Y, arguing that it increases efficiency and productivity.

The research of McGregor and his successors ultimately led to a new way of thinking about how organizations should behave: contingency theory,* which calls for management to adapt an organization's needs and economic aims to the economy and culture of the society in which it exists. Companies should become "learning organizations"* through the application of Theory Y principles, so that they can adapt to new, changing, and dynamic markets.

We can see, then, that even though McGregor died in 1964, his work continues to influence both businesses and those who study them.

1. Thomas C. Head, "Douglas McGregor's Legacy: Lessons Learned, Lessons Lost," *Journal of Management History* 17, no. 2 (2011): 202–16.

2. William P. Anthony, K. Michele Kacmar and Pamela L. Perrewe, *Human Resource Management: A Strategic Approach* (Mason, OH: Thomson/South-Western, 2006).

3. Monica Kirkpatrick Johnson, Rayna Amber Sage, and Jeylan T. Mortimer, "Work Values, Early Career Difficulties, and the U. S. Economic Recession," *Social Psychology Quarterly* 75, no. 3 (2012): 242–67.

4. Douglas McGregor, *The Human Side of Enterprise* (New York: McGraw-Hill, 1960), 41.

5. Paul Attewell, "Big Brother and the Sweatshop: Computer Surveillance in the Automated Office," *Sociological Theory* 5 (1987): 87–100.

GLOSSARY OF TERMS

1. **Alfred P. Sloan Foundation:** a not-for-profit organization. It was founded in 1934 by Alfred Pritchard Sloan Jr., who spent his career as an executive at the automobile company General Motors. Sloan's purpose for his foundation was to provide grants for innovative research in science and technology.

2. **Behavioral management:** a type of management that emphasizes the human dimension of work. It views human beings as individual resources who have potential for growth. It is also known as the human relations movement.

3. **Behaviorism:** the theory that human behavior offers important insights into human psychology, and that it can be measured, trained, and changed.

4. **Contingency theory:** a management theory based on the belief that decisions and leadership are dependent upon the environment in which the organization operates.

5. **Cost-reduction sharing:** a policy in which employees share the financial rewards of an organization's success (increased productivity or decreased production costs, for example). Employees receive monthly bonuses on top of their basic wages.

6. **Cross-cultural psychology:** a branch of psychology that examines psychological differences and similarities across cultural borders.

7. **Electronic sweatshops:** places of work in which employees are constantly monitored by the management using computer surveillance. "Sweatshop" itself is a term for a business in which employees are exploited and have to work long hours for little pay.

8. **Great Depression:** the decade following the 1929 stock market crash, during which millions of Americans could not find work and lived in poverty.

9. **Great Recession:** the collapse of the financial markets in the United States between 2007 and 2009 that left millions of Americans unemployed. At the height of the Great Recession, the unemployment rate was nearly 10 percent.

10. **Group dynamics:** the study of how humans behave in groups. First coined by the psychologist Kurt Lewin.

11. **Hierarchy of needs:** a concept developed by the psychologist Abraham Maslow to describe and rank different types of human motivation. The pyramid of needs that he identified ranged from basic physiological needs (the need for

food and shelter), through to the need for fulfillment and self-actualization.

12. **Humanism:** a philosophy that holds that individual human beings should have the opportunity to realize their full potential. From a business perspective, humanistic working conditions combine both employees' needs and the company's goals in order to achieve higher efficiency.

13. **Learning organization:** a learning organization is rooted in the idea that there is no best form of management. Such an organization has the flexibility to adapt to its environment (economic and cultural) through a shared vision of all employees, and a focus on team learning.

14. **Management by Objectives (MBO):** a system whereby managers and employees collaborate to develop objectives and plans. These plans are regularly monitored to ensure that they remain on track.

15. **McGregor Institute:** a charitable organization dedicated to helping people who are struggling to find work. It was founded in 1895 by Douglas McGregor's grandfather.

16. **Organizational behaviorists:** those engaged in the systemic study of the function of organizations, using behaviorist assumptions and methods.

17. **Organizational development (OD):** an academic field focused on understanding and managing organizational change. Kurt Lewin is generally seen as the father of organizational development.

18. **Organizational psychology:** the systematic study of how the workplace affects the human mind.

19. **Natural soldiering:** the tendency of workers to take it easy while working.

20. **Postwar period:** the period of adjustment after World War II, when millions of soldiers returned to the United States, and Europe had to rebuild itself.

21. **Psychoanalysis:** a therapeutic method and theoretical approach to the behavioral phenomena and conditions provoked by unconscious thought.

22. **Referent power:** a term coined by management scholars Daniel Katz and Robert Kahn to describe the power that managers obtain from being liked by their subordinates.

23. **Scanlon Plan:** a plan developed by the unionist and steelworker Joseph Scanlon in the 1930s to help businesses cope with the economic climate. The plan called for businesses to draw on the potential of their employees, and for employee collaboration.

24. **Scientific management:** the idea that organizations can be managed on the basis of scientific principles. It is also known as "Taylorism" after the industrialist and early management scholar Frederick Winslow Taylor.

25. **Self-actualization:** the fulfillment of an individual's creative potential.

26. **Self-initiative:** the ability of employees to start work without being told by managers what to do.

27. **Staff-line relationships:** a term describing the relationship between superiors (staff) and their employees/subordinates (line). It originally referred to managers and employees working in an assembly-line setting.

28. **Systematic soldiering:** the idea that when one or more employees perform the absolute minimum required by their job, other employees will also begin to do as little as possible.

29. **Theory X:** a management theory based on the assumption that people are idle and will operate only under strict control or for monetary incentives. It describes traditional management principles, based on Sigmund Freud's psychoanalysis and F. W. Taylor's scientific management principles.

30. **Theory Y:** a management theory that assumes people are self-motivated and do not need to be strictly controlled. Under Theory Y's assumptions, employees want to work hard in order to learn and grow.

31. **Theory Z:** a theory developed by William G. Ouchi based on the success of Japanese businesses. It suggests that American businesses should draw on Eastern management styles, which value (among other things) employee well-being.

32. **Uncertainty avoidance:** the degree to which people in a given country or culture accept unexpected situations, uncertainty, and ambiguity. The notion of uncertainty avoidance was developed by the Dutch cross-cultural psychologist Geert Hofstede.

►►⟩— PEOPLE MENTIONED IN THE TEXT —⟨◄◄

1. **Theodore M. Alfred (1925–2007)** was a professor of management policy at Case Western Reserve University in Cleveland, Ohio; he received a PhD in Industrial Economics from the Massachusetts Institute of Technology (MIT), where he collaborated with Douglas McGregor.

2. **Chris Argyris (1923–2013)** was an American business theorist and professor at Harvard Business School who focused on behavior in organizations.

3. **Alex Bavelas (b. 1920)** is an American psychologist and professor of business management at the Massachusetts Institute of Technology (MIT), where he started a group networks laboratory.

4. **Peter Drucker (1909–2005)** was an Austrian-born American lecturer and management consultant. His books included *Concept of the Corporation* (1972) and *Management: Tasks, Responsibilities, and Practices* (1974).

5. **Mary Parker Follett (1868–1933)** was a social worker who later became a management theorist. She is seen as a pioneer in organizational theory and organizational behavior.

6. **Sigmund Freud (1856–1939)** was an Austrian neurologist. He is famed for founding psychoanalysis, a therapeutic and theoretical model for the treatment of psychological disorders by addressing patients' unconscious conflicts.

7. **Geert Hofstede (b. 1928)** is a Dutch social psychologist who focuses on cross-cultural groups and organizations. He is well known for developing the cultural dimensions theory.

8. **Robert L. Kahn (b. 1918)** is an American psychologist who specializes in organizational theory and survey research. He co-authored *The Social Psychology of Organizations* with Daniel Katz, which was published in 1966.

9. **Daniel Katz (1903–98)** was an American psychologist and an expert in organizational psychology. He was a professor at the University of Michigan and is best known for his 1966 book, *The Social Psychology of Organizations*.

10. **Anthony Lerner** is an external organization development consultant and a principal at Arthur Lerner Associates.

11. **Kurt Lewin (1890–1947)** was a pioneering German American psychologist in the fields of social and organizational psychology. He contributed research on group dynamics and organizational development.

12. **Abraham Maslow (1908–70)** was an American psychologist who developed what became known as Maslow's hierarchy of needs.

13. **Elton Mayo (1880–1949)** was an Australian psychologist, organizational theorist, and industrial researcher who studied the behavior of people in groups.

14. **William G. Ouchi (b. 1943)** is a professor of management and organizations at the University of California Los Angeles' Anderson School of Management. He is well known for his book *Theory Z* (1981), in which he proposes that a combination of Eastern and Western styles of management would benefit American business corporations.

15. **Joseph Scanlon (1899–1956)** was a steelworker and local union president who invented the Scanlon Plan, which was based on cost-reduction sharing and employee participation. He was invited by Douglas McGregor to become a lecturer at the Massachusetts Institute of Technology.

16. **Edgar Schein (b. 1928)** is a former professor at the Massachusetts Institute of Technology, a colleague of Douglas McGregor, and a social psychologist who published work about corporate culture.

17. **Peter Senge (b. 1947)** is a management theorist and senior lecturer at the Massachusetts Institute of Technology's School of Management. He founded the Society for Organizational Learning.

18. **B. F. Skinner (1904–90)** was an American psychologist and behaviorist who taught at Harvard University. He is generally seen as a key figure in the development of modern behaviorism.

19. **Alfred P. Sloan (1875–1966)** was a wealthy automotive business executive who established the School of Industrial Management at the Massachusetts Institute of Technology in 1952.

20. **Frederick Winslow Taylor (1856–1915)** was an engineer who is credited with developing the theory and practice of scientific management, which became the basis for classical organizational theory.

21. **John B. Watson (1878–1958)** was an American psychologist who founded the psychological school of behaviorism.

22. **Joan Woodward (1916–71)** was a British professor in organization sociology at Imperial College London.

# WORKS CITED

1. Anthony, William P., K. Michele Kacmar, and Pamela L. Perrewe. *Human Resource Management: A Strategic Approach*. Mason, OH: Thomson/South-Western, 2006.

2. Argyris, Chris. *Teaching Smart People How to Learn*. Boston, MA: Harvard Business Press, 1998.

3. Attewell, Paul. "Big Brother and the Sweatshop: Computer Surveillance in the Automated Office." *Sociological Theory* 5 (1987): 87–100.

4. Babcock, Richard. "Tracing the History of MBO." In *Strategies and Tactics in Management by Objectives,* edited by Richard Babcock and Peter F. Sorensen, 2–24. Champaign, IL: Stipes, 1976.

5. Bennis, Warren. "Chairman Mac in Perspective." *Journal of Management History* 17, no. 2 (2011): 1–11.

6. Burke, W. Warren. "The Douglas McGregor Legacy." *Journal of Applied Behavioral Science* 45 (2009): 8–11.

7. ____. *Organization Change: Theory and Practice*. Thousand Oaks, CA: Sage, 2008.

8. Burns, Tom, and George M. Stalker. *The Management of Innovation*. London: Tavistock, 1961.

9. Business Dictionary. "Scanlon Plan." Accessed November 20, 2015. www.businessdictionary.com/definition/scanlon-plan.html.

10. Cunningham, Robert A. "Douglas McGregor: A Lasting Impression." *Ivey Business Journal* 75 (2011): 5–7.

11. Freud, Sigmund. "An Outline of Psycho-analysis." *International Journal of Psychoanalysis* 21 (1940): 27–84.

12. Guetzkow, Harold. Review of *Leadership and Organization: A Behavioral Science Approach* by Robert Tannenbaum, Irving R. Weschler, and Fred Massarik. *American Sociological Review* 26, no. 5 (1961): 804.

13. Head, Thomas C. "Douglas McGregor's Legacy: Lessons Learned, Lessons Lost." *Journal of Management History* 17, no. 2 (2011): 202–16.

14. Heil, Gary, Warren Bennis, and Deborah C. Stephens. *Douglas McGregor, Revisited: Managing the Human Side of the Enterprise.* New York: Wiley, 2000.

15. Hellriegel, Don, Susan E. Jackson, and John W. Slocum. *Management: A*

Competency-Based Approach. Cincinnati, OH: South-Western Publishing, 2002.

16. Hindle, Tim. *Guide to Management Ideas and Gurus*. London: Profile Books, 2008.

17. Jacobs, David. "Book Review Essay: Douglas McGregor: The Human Side of Enterprise in Peril." *Academy of Management Review* 29, no. 2 (2004): 293–6.

18. Johnson, Monica Kirkpatrick, Rayna Amber Sage, and Jeylan T. Mortimer. "Work Values, Early Career Difficulties, and the U. S. Economic Recession." *Social Psychology Quarterly* 75, no. 3 (2012): 242–67.

19. Katz, Daniel, and Robert L. Kahn. *The Social Psychology of Organizations*. New York: John Wiley & Sons, 1966.

20. Kermally, Sultan. *Gurus on People Management*. London: Thorogood, 2004.

21. Lawrence, Paul R., and Jay William Lorsch. "High Performing Organizations in Three Environments." In *Organization and Environment: Managing Differentiation and Integration*, edited by Paul R. Lawrence and Jay William Lorsch, 133–58. Boston, MA: Harvard Business School, 1967.

22. Lerner, Arthur. "McGregor's Legacy: Thoughts on What He Left, What Transpired, and What Remains to Pursue." *Journal of Management History* 17, no. 2 (2011): 217–37.

23. Likert, Rensis. *The Human Organization: Its Management and Value*. New York: McGraw-Hill, 1967.

24. "Management by Objectives." *Economist*, Accessed November 20, 2015. www. economist.com/node/14299761.

25. Managers-Net. "Douglas McGregor." Accessed November 19, 2015. www. managers-net.com/biography/mcgregor.html.

26. _____. "George Elton Mayo." Accessed November 20, 2015. www. managers-net. com/Biography/Mayo.html.

27. Maslow, Abraham H. *Eupsychian Management: A Journal*. Homewood, IL: Irwin, 1965.

28. _____. *Motivation and Personality*. New York: Harper & Row, 1954.

29. _____. "A Theory of Human Motivation." *Psychological Review* 50 (1943): 370–96.

30. McGregor, Douglas. "The Human Side of Enterprise." First published in

Adventure in Thought and Action: Proceedings of the Fifth Anniversary Convocation of the School of Industrial Management, Massachusetts Institute of Technology, Cambridge, April 9, 1957. Cambridge, MA: MIT School of Industrial Management, 1957. Reprinted in *The Management Review* 46 (1957): 22–8.

31. ____. *The Human Side of Enterprise*. New York: McGraw-Hill, 1960.

32. ____. *The Professional Manager*. New York: McGraw-Hill, 1967.

33. McGregor Fund, "History." Accessed November 19, 2015. www.mcgregorfund. org/about-us/history.

34. Mind Tools Editorial Team. "Theory Z: Merging Eastern and Western Management Styles." Accessed November 24, 2015. www.mindtools.com/pages/ article/theory-z.htm.

35. MIT Sloan School of Management. "Pioneered at MIT Sloan." Accessed November 19, 2015. mitsloan.mit.edu/faculty/spotlight/pioneered.php.

36. Ouchi, William G. *Theory Z: How American Business Can Meet the Japanese Challenge*. Reading, MA: Addison-Wesley, 1981.

37. Sanchez, Carol M., and Dawn M. Curtis, "Different Minds and Common Problems: Geert Hofstede's Research on National Cultures." *Performance Improvement Quarterly* 13, no. 2 (2000): 9–19.

38. Schein, Edgar. "In Defense of Theory Y." *Organizational Dynamics* 4 (1975): 17–30.

39. ____. "Relationships between Sex Role Stereotypes and Requisite Management Characteristics among Female Managers." *Journal of Applied Psychology* 60, no. 3 (1975): 340–4.

40. Senge, Peter. *The Fifth Discipline: The Art and Practice of the Learning Organization.* New York: Doubleday, 1990.

41. ____. "The Practice of Innovation." *Leader to Leader* 9 (1998): 16–22.

42. Sorensen, Peter F., and Matt Minahan. "McGregor's Legacy: The Evolution and Current Application of Theory Y Management." *Journal of Management History* 17, no. 2 (2011): 178–92.

43. Taylor, Frederick Winslow. "Fundamentals of Scientific Management." In *Working in America: Continuity, Conflict, and Change*, edited by Amy S. Wharton, 67–75. Mountain View, CA: Mayfield Publishing Company, 1998.

44. "The 25 Most Influential Business Management Books." *Time*. Accessed November 20, 2015. http://content.time.com/time/specials/packages/completelist/0,29569,2086680,00.html.

45. Vaill, Peter B. "Process Wisdom for a New Age." *ReVISION* 7, no. 2 (1986): 39–49.

46. Waterman, Robert H. *The Frontiers of Excellence: Learning from Companies That Put People First*. London: Nicholas Brealey Publishing, 1994.

47. Watson, John B. "Psychology as the Behaviorist Views It." *Psychological Review* 20 (1913): 158–77.

48. Woodward, Joan. *Industrial Organization: Theory and Practice*. New York: Oxford University Press, 1965.

原书作者简介

1906 年，道格拉斯·麦格雷戈出生于美国底特律。青年时代目睹了 20 世纪 30 年代美国经济大萧条的各种影响后，麦格雷戈立志要为困境中的人们改善生活，并尽力去研究什么样的工作条件能让工作更吸引人、更有意义。1935 年，麦格雷戈取得哈佛大学的博士学位，随后受聘于著名的麻省理工学院。作为一名专门从事社会心理学和组织心理学的教师，麦格雷戈在其职业生涯中致力于工作满意度的研究，其思想对商业学者产生了极为深远的影响。1964 年，麦格雷戈逝世，享年 58 岁。

本书作者简介

斯托扬·斯托扬诺夫博士，爱丁堡大学管理学博士，现任格拉斯哥市的思克莱德大学亨特创业研究中心讲师。

莫妮卡·狄德瑞奇博士，格罗宁根大学心理学硕士、内华达大学拉斯维加斯分校社会学博士。

世界名著中的批判性思维

《世界思想宝库钥匙丛书》致力于深入浅出地阐释全世界著名思想家的观点，不论是谁、在何处都能了解到，从而推进批判性思维发展。

《世界思想宝库钥匙丛书》与世界顶尖大学的一流学者合作，为一系列学科中最有影响的著作推出新的分析文本，介绍其观点和影响。在这一不断扩展的系列中，每种选入的著作都代表了历经时间考验的思想典范。通过为这些著作提供必要背景、揭示原作者的学术渊源以及说明这些著作所产生的影响，本系列图书希望让读者以新视角看待这些划时代的经典之作。读者应学会思考、运用并挑战这些著作中的观点，而不是简单接受它们。

ABOUT THE AUTHOR OF THE ORIGINAL WORK

Douglas McGregor was born in Detroit in the United States in 1906. As a young man, he witnessed the effects of the Great Depression—the economic downturn of the 1930s. McGregor wanted to improve the lives of those who experienced adversity and tried to understand the kind of conditions that could make work enjoyable and meaningful. He received his doctorate from Harvard in 1935, and was eventually hired by the prestigious Massachusetts Institute of Technology. As a faculty member specializing in social and organizational psychology, McGregor dedicated his career to studying what makes work satisfying, and his thinking has had a great influence on business scholars. Douglas McGregor died in 1964 at the age of 58.

ABOUT THE AUTHORS OF THE ANALYSIS

Dr Stoyan Stoyanov holds a PhD in management from the University of Edinburgh. He is currently a lecturer at the Hunter Centre for Entrepreneurship at the University of Strathclyde, Glasgow.

Dr Monique Diderich holds a masters degree in psychology from the University of Groningen and a doctorate in sociology from the University of Nevada, Las Vegas.

ABOUT MACAT
GREAT WORKS FOR CRITICAL THINKING

Macat is focused on making the ideas of the world's great thinkers accessible and comprehensible to everybody, everywhere, in ways that promote the development of enhanced critical thinking skills.

It works with leading academics from the world's top universities to produce new analyses that focus on the ideas and the impact of the most influential works ever written across a wide variety of academic disciplines. Each of the works that sit at the heart of its growing library is an enduring example of great thinking. But by setting them in context—and looking at the influences that shaped their authors, as well as the responses they provoked—Macat encourages readers to look at these classics and game-changers with fresh eyes. Readers learn to think, engage and challenge their ideas, rather than simply accepting them.

批判性思维与《企业的人性面》

首要批判性思维技巧：评估

次要批判性思维技巧：理性化思维

一个优秀经理人应该具有什么素质？尽管我们都能指出某人是我们认为的优秀经理人，但究竟是什么因素使得他们对管理工作得心应手？这个问题很复杂，而且对于改进企业组织而言也是至关重要。管理学者道格拉斯·麦格雷戈于1960年出版的开创性著作《企业的人性面》可能是回答这一问题的最有影响力的尝试，该书也很好地说明了强大的评估、推理技能是如何生效的。

评估是一种需要判断各种看法之优缺点的批判性思维技能：批判性评估着眼于推理过程的可接受程度以及论据的适当性、相关性和说服力。麦格雷戈试图通过分析不同管理方法、其对人类行为的假设以及其效果，从而发现优秀经理人的要素。他认为管理方法大致可分为两种"理论"：对员工动机抱有消极看法的X理论和对员工动机抱有积极假设的Y理论。麦格雷戈的评估显示，Y理论在生产效率和其他可测量指标上产生明显更好的效果。在此基础上，麦格雷戈推出了令人信服的论点：大规模采用Y理论的策略。

CRITICAL THINKING AND *THE HUMAN SIDE OF ENTERPRISE*

- Primary critical thinking skill: EVALUATION
- Secondary critical thinking skill: REASONING

What makes a good manager? Though we can probably all point to someone we think of as a good manager, what precisely makes them so good at their job is a complex question-and one central to good business organization. Management scholar Douglas McGregor's seminal 1960 book *The Human Side of Enterprise* is perhaps the most influential attempt to answer that question, and provides an excellent example of strong evaluative and reasoning skills in action.

Evaluation is a critical thinking skill that requires judging the strength and weakness of positions: a critical evaluation asks how acceptable a line of reasoning is, and how adequate, relevant and convincing the evidence is. McGregor sought to find out what makes a good manager by evaluating different management approaches, their assumptions about human behavior, and effects they had. In his view, management approaches could be roughly broken down into two "theories": Theory X, which held a negative idea of employee motivations; and Theory Y, which made positive assumptions about them. McGregor's evaluation showed that Theory Y produced markedly better results in productivity and other measurable areas. On this basis, McGregor reasoned out a strong, persuasive argument for adopting Theory Y strategies on a grand scale.

《世界思想宝库钥匙丛书》简介

《世界思想宝库钥匙丛书》致力于为一系列在各领域产生重大影响的人文社科类经典著作提供独特的学术探讨。每一本读物都不仅仅是原经典著作的内容摘要，而是介绍并深入研究原经典著作的学术渊源、主要观点和历史影响。这一丛书的目的是提供一套学习资料，以促进读者掌握批判性思维，从而更全面、深刻地去理解重要思想。

每一本读物分为 3 个部分：学术渊源、学术思想和学术影响，每个部分下有 4 个小节。这些章节旨在从各个方面研究原经典著作及其反响。

由于独特的体例，每一本读物不但易于阅读，而且另有一项优点：所有读物的编排体例相同，读者在进行某个知识层面的调查或研究时可交叉参阅多本该丛书中的相关读物，从而开启跨领域研究的路径。

为了方便阅读，每本读物最后还列出了术语表和人名表（在书中则以星号 * 标记），此外还有参考文献。

《世界思想宝库钥匙丛书》与剑桥大学合作，理清了批判性思维的要点，即如何通过 6 种技能来进行有效思考。其中 3 种技能让我们能够理解问题，另 3 种技能让我们有能力解决问题。这 6 种技能合称为"批判性思维 PACIER 模式"，它们是：

分析：了解如何建立一个观点；
评估：研究一个观点的优点和缺点；
阐释：对意义所产生的问题加以理解；
创造性思维：提出新的见解，发现新的联系；
解决问题：提出切实有效的解决办法；
理性化思维：创建有说服力的观点。

THE MACAT LIBRARY

The Macat Library is a series of unique academic explorations of seminal works in the humanities and social sciences — books and papers that have had a significant and widely recognised impact on their disciplines. It has been created to serve as much more than just a summary of what lies between the covers of a great book. It illuminates and explores the influences on, ideas of, and impact of that book. Our goal is to offer a learning resource that encourages critical thinking and fosters a better, deeper understanding of important ideas.

Each publication is divided into three Sections: Influences, Ideas, and Impact. Each Section has four Modules. These explore every important facet of the work, and the responses to it.

This Section-Module structure makes a Macat Library book easy to use, but it has another important feature. Because each Macat book is written to the same format, it is possible (and encouraged!) to cross-reference multiple Macat books along the same lines of inquiry or research. This allows the reader to open up interesting interdisciplinary pathways.

To further aid your reading, lists of glossary terms and people mentioned are included at the end of this book (these are indicated by an asterisk [*] throughout) — as well as a list of works cited.

Macat has worked with the University of Cambridge to identify the elements of critical thinking and understand the ways in which six different skills combine to enable effective thinking.

Three allow us to fully understand a problem; three more give us the tools to solve it. Together, these six skills make up the PACIER model of critical thinking. They are:

ANALYSIS — understanding how an argument is built
EVALUATION — exploring the strengths and weaknesses of an argument
INTERPRETATION — understanding issues of meaning
CREATIVE THINKING — coming up with new ideas and fresh connections
PROBLEM-SOLVING — producing strong solutions
REASONING — creating strong arguments

"《世界思想宝库钥匙丛书》提供了独一无二的跨学科学习和研究工具。它介绍那些革新了各自学科研究的经典著作，还邀请全世界一流专家和教育机构进行严谨的分析，为每位读者打开世界顶级教育的大门。"

—— 安德烈亚斯·施莱歇尔，
经济合作与发展组织教育与技能司司长

"《世界思想宝库钥匙丛书》直面大学教育的巨大挑战……他们组建了一支精干而活跃的学者队伍，来推出在研究广度上颇具新意的教学材料。"

—— 布罗尔斯教授、勋爵，剑桥大学前校长

"《世界思想宝库钥匙丛书》的愿景令人赞叹。它通过分析和阐释那些曾深刻影响人类思想以及社会、经济发展的经典文本，提供了新的学习方法。它推动批判性思维，这对于任何社会和经济体来说都是至关重要的。这就是未来的学习方法。"

—— 查尔斯·克拉克阁下，英国前教育大臣

"对于那些影响了各自领域的著作，《世界思想宝库钥匙丛书》能让人们立即了解到围绕那些著作展开的评论性言论，这让该系列图书成为在这些领域从事研究的师生们不可或缺的资源。"

—— 威廉·特朗佐教授，加利福尼亚大学圣地亚哥分校

"Macat offers an amazing first-of-its-kind tool for interdisciplinary learning and research. Its focus on works that transformed their disciplines and its rigorous approach, drawing on the world's leading experts and educational institutions, opens up a world-class education to anyone."

—— Andreas Schleicher, Director for Education and Skills, Organisation for Economic Co-operation and Development

"Macat is taking on some of the major challenges in university education... They have drawn together a strong team of active academics who are producing teaching materials that are novel in the breadth of their approach."

—— Prof Lord Broers, former Vice-Chancellor of the University of Cambridge

"The Macat vision is exceptionally exciting. It focuses upon new modes of learning which analyse and explain seminal texts which have profoundly influenced world thinking and so social and economic development. It promotes the kind of critical thinking which is essential for any society and economy. This is the learning of the future."

—— Rt Hon Charles Clarke, former UK Secretary of State for Education

"The Macat analyses provide immediate access to the critical conversation surrounding the books that have shaped their respective discipline, which will make them an invaluable resource to all of those, students and teachers, working in the field."

—— Prof William Tronzo, University of California at San Diego

The Macat Library
世界思想宝库钥匙丛书

TITLE	中文书名	类别
An Analysis of Arjun Appadurai's *Modernity at Large: Cultural Dimensions of Globalization*	解析阿尔君·阿帕杜莱《消失的现代性：全球化的文化维度》	人类学
An Analysis of Claude Lévi-Strauss's *Structural Anthropology*	解析克劳德·列维-斯特劳斯《结构人类学》	人类学
An Analysis of Marcel Mauss's *The Gift*	解析马塞尔·莫斯《礼物》	人类学
An Analysis of Jared M. Diamond's *Guns, Germs, and Steel: The Fate of Human Societies*	解析贾雷德·戴蒙德《枪炮、病菌与钢铁：人类社会的命运》	人类学
An Analysis of Clifford Geertz's *The Interpretation of Cultures*	解析克利福德·格尔茨《文化的解释》	人类学
An Analysis of Philippe Ariès's *Centuries of Childhood: A Social History of Family Life*	解析菲力浦·阿利埃斯《儿童的世纪：旧制度下的儿童和家庭生活》	人类学
An Analysis of W. Chan Kim & Renée Mauborgne's *Blue Ocean Strategy*	解析金伟灿/勒妮·莫博涅《蓝海战略》	商业
An Analysis of John P. Kotter's *Leading Change*	解析约翰·P.科特《领导变革》	商业
An Analysis of Michael E. Porter's *Competitive Strategy: Techniques for Analyzing Industries and Competitors*	解析迈克尔·E.波特《竞争战略：分析产业和竞争对手的技术》	商业
An Analysis of Jean Lave & Etienne Wenger's *Situated Learning: Legitimate Peripheral Participation*	解析琼·莱夫/艾蒂纳·温格《情境学习：合法的边缘性参与》	商业
An Analysis of Douglas McGregor's *The Human Side of Enterprise*	解析道格拉斯·麦格雷戈《企业的人性面》	商业
An Analysis of Milton Friedman's *Capitalism and Freedom*	解析米尔顿·弗里德曼《资本主义与自由》	商业
An Analysis of Ludwig von Mises's *The Theory of Money and Credit*	解析路德维希·冯·米塞斯《货币和信用理论》	经济学
An Analysis of Adam Smith's *The Wealth of Nations*	解析亚当·斯密《国富论》	经济学
An Analysis of Thomas Piketty's *Capital in the Twenty-First Century*	解析托马斯·皮凯蒂《21世纪资本论》	经济学
An Analysis of Nassim Nicholas Taleb's *The Black Swan: The Impact of the Highly Improbable*	解析纳西姆·尼古拉斯·塔勒布《黑天鹅：如何应对不可预知的未来》	经济学
An Analysis of Ha-Joon Chang's *Kicking Away the Ladder*	解析张夏准《富国陷阱：发达国家为何踢开梯子》	经济学
An Analysis of Thomas Robert Malthus's *An Essay on the Principle of Population*	解析托马斯·马尔萨斯《人口论》	经济学

An Analysis of John Maynard Keynes's *The General Theory of Employment, Interest and Money*	解析约翰·梅纳德·凯恩斯《就业、利息和货币通论》	经济学
An Analysis of Milton Friedman's *The Role of Monetary Policy*	解析米尔顿·弗里德曼《货币政策的作用》	经济学
An Analysis of Burton G. Malkiel's *A Random Walk Down Wall Street*	解析伯顿·G.马尔基尔《漫步华尔街》	经济学
An Analysis of Friedrich A. Hayek's *The Road to Serfdom*	解析弗里德里希·A.哈耶克《通往奴役之路》	经济学
An Analysis of Charles P. Kindleberger's *Manias, Panics, and Crashes: A History of Financial Crises*	解析查尔斯·P.金德尔伯格《疯狂、惊恐和崩溃：金融危机史》	经济学
An Analysis of Amartya Sen's *Development as Freedom*	解析阿马蒂亚·森《以自由看待发展》	经济学
An Analysis of Rachel Carson's *Silent Spring*	解析蕾切尔·卡森《寂静的春天》	地理学
An Analysis of Charles Darwin's *On the Origin of Species: by Means of Natural Selection, or The Preservation of Favoured Races in the Struggle for Life*	解析查尔斯·达尔文《物种起源》	地理学
An Analysis of World Commission on Environment and Development's *The Brundtland Report, Our Common Future*	解析世界环境与发展委员会《布伦特兰报告：我们共同的未来》	地理学
An Analysis of James E. Lovelock's *Gaia: A New Look at Life on Earth*	解析詹姆斯·E.拉伍洛克《盖娅：地球生命的新视野》	地理学
An Analysis of Paul Kennedy's *The Rise and Fall of the Great Powers: Economic Change and Military Conflict from 1500—2000*	解析保罗·肯尼迪《大国的兴衰：1500—2000年的经济变革与军事冲突》	历史
An Analysis of Janet L. Abu-Lughod's *Before European Hegemony: The World System A. D. 1250—1350*	解析珍妮特·L.阿布-卢格霍德《欧洲霸权之前：1250—1350年的世界体系》	历史
An Analysis of Alfred W. Crosby's *The Columbian Exchange: Biological and Cultural Consequences of 1492*	解析艾尔弗雷德·W.克罗斯比《哥伦布大交换：1492年以后的生物影响和文化冲击》	历史
An Analysis of Tony Judt's *Postwar: A History of Europe since 1945*	解析托尼·朱特《战后欧洲史》	历史
An Analysis of Richard J. Evans's *In Defence of History*	解析理查德·J.艾文斯《捍卫历史》	历史
An Analysis of Eric Hobsbawm's *The Age of Revolution: Europe 1789–1848*	解析艾瑞克·霍布斯鲍姆《革命的年代：欧洲1789—1848年》	历史

An Analysis of Roland Barthes's *Mythologies*	解析罗兰·巴特《神话学》	文学与批判理论
An Analysis of Simone de Beauvoir's *The Second Sex*	解析西蒙娜·德·波伏娃《第二性》	文学与批判理论
An Analysis of Edward W. Said's *Orientalism*	解析爱德华·W.萨义德《东方主义》	文学与批判理论
An Analysis of Virginia Woolf's *A Room of One's Own*	解析弗吉尼亚·伍尔芙《一间自己的房间》	文学与批判理论
An Analysis of Judith Butler's *Gender Trouble*	解析朱迪斯·巴特勒《性别麻烦》	文学与批判理论
An Analysis of Ferdinand de Saussure's *Course in General Linguistics*	解析费尔迪南·德·索绪尔《普通语言学教程》	文学与批判理论
An Analysis of Susan Sontag's *On Photography*	解析苏珊·桑塔格《论摄影》	文学与批判理论
An Analysis of Walter Benjamin's *The Work of Art in the Age of Mechanical Reproduction*	解析瓦尔特·本雅明《机械复制时代的艺术作品》	文学与批判理论
An Analysis of W.E.B. Du Bois's *The Souls of Black Folk*	解析W.E.B.杜波依斯《黑人的灵魂》	文学与批判理论
An Analysis of Plato's *The Republic*	解析柏拉图《理想国》	哲学
An Analysis of Plato's *Symposium*	解析柏拉图《会饮篇》	哲学
An Analysis of Aristotle's *Metaphysics*	解析亚里士多德《形而上学》	哲学
An Analysis of Aristotle's *Nicomachean Ethics*	解析亚里士多德《尼各马可伦理学》	哲学
An Analysis of Immanuel Kant's *Critique of Pure Reason*	解析伊曼努尔·康德《纯粹理性批判》	哲学
An Analysis of Ludwig Wittgenstein's *Philosophical Investigations*	解析路德维希·维特根斯坦《哲学研究》	哲学
An Analysis of G.W.F. Hegel's *Phenomenology of Spirit*	解析G.W.F.黑格尔《精神现象学》	哲学
An Analysis of Baruch Spinoza's *Ethics*	解析巴鲁赫·斯宾诺莎《伦理学》	哲学
An Analysis of Hannah Arendt's *The Human Condition*	解析汉娜·阿伦特《人的境况》	哲学
An Analysis of G.E.M. Anscombe's *Modern Moral Philosophy*	解析G.E.M.安斯康姆《现代道德哲学》	哲学
An Analysis of David Hume's *An Enquiry Concerning Human Understanding*	解析大卫·休谟《人类理解研究》	哲学

An Analysis of Søren Kierkegaard's *Fear and Trembling*	解析索伦·克尔凯郭尔《恐惧与战栗》	哲学
An Analysis of René Descartes's *Meditations on First Philosophy*	解析勒内·笛卡尔《第一哲学沉思录》	哲学
An Analysis of Friedrich Nietzsche's *On the Genealogy of Morality*	解析弗里德里希·尼采《论道德的谱系》	哲学
An Analysis of Gilbert Ryle's *The Concept of Mind*	解析吉尔伯特·赖尔《心的概念》	哲学
An Analysis of Thomas Kuhn's *The Structure of Scientific Revolutions*	解析托马斯·库恩《科学革命的结构》	哲学
An Analysis of John Stuart Mill's *Utilitarianism*	解析约翰·斯图亚特·穆勒《功利主义》	哲学
An Analysis of Aristotle's *Politics*	解析亚里士多德《政治学》	政治学
An Analysis of Niccolò Machiavelli's *The Prince*	解析尼科洛·马基雅维利《君主论》	政治学
An Analysis of Karl Marx's *Capital*	解析卡尔·马克思《资本论》	政治学
An Analysis of Benedict Anderson's *Imagined Communities*	解析本尼迪克特·安德森《想象的共同体》	政治学
An Analysis of Samuel P. Huntington's *The Clash of Civilizations and the Remaking of World Order*	解析塞缪尔·P.亨廷顿《文明的冲突与世界秩序重建》	政治学
An Analysis of Alexis de Tocqueville's *Democracy in America*	解析阿列克西·德·托克维尔《论美国的民主》	政治学
An Analysis of John A. Hobson's *Imperialism: A Study*	解析约翰·A.霍布森《帝国主义》	政治学
An Analysis of Thomas Paine's *Common Sense*	解析托马斯·潘恩《常识》	政治学
An Analysis of John Rawls's *A Theory of Justice*	解析约翰·罗尔斯《正义论》	政治学
An Analysis of Francis Fukuyama's *The End of History and the Last Man*	解析弗朗西斯·福山《历史的终结与最后的人》	政治学
An Analysis of John Locke's *Two Treatises of Government*	解析约翰·洛克《政府论》	政治学
An Analysis of Sun Tzu's *The Art of War*	解析孙武《孙子兵法》	政治学
An Analysis of Henry Kissinger's *World Order: Reflections on the Character of Nations and the Course of History*	解析亨利·基辛格《世界秩序》	政治学
An Analysis of Jean-Jacques Rousseau's *The Social Contract*	解析让-雅克·卢梭《社会契约论》	政治学

An Analysis of Odd Arne Westad's *The Global Cold War: Third World Interventions and the Making of Our Times*	解析文安立《全球冷战：美苏对第三世界的干涉与当代世界的形成》	政治学
An Analysis of Sigmund Freud's *The Interpretation of Dreams*	解析西格蒙德·弗洛伊德《梦的解析》	心理学
An Analysis of William James' *The Principles of Psychology*	解析威廉·詹姆斯《心理学原理》	心理学
An Analysis of Philip Zimbardo's *The Lucifer Effect*	解析菲利普·津巴多《路西法效应》	心理学
An Analysis of Leon Festinger's *A Theory of Cognitive Dissonance*	解析利昂·费斯汀格《认知失调论》	心理学
An Analysis of Richard H. Thaler & Cass R. Sunstein's *Nudge: Improving Decisions about Health, Wealth, and Happiness*	解析理查德·H.泰勒/卡斯·R.桑斯坦《助推：如何做出有关健康、财富和幸福的更优决策》	心理学
An Analysis of Gordon Allport's *The Nature of Prejudice*	解析高尔登·奥尔波特《偏见的本质》	心理学
An Analysis of Steven Pinker's *The Better Angels of Our Nature: Why Violence Has Declined*	解析斯蒂芬·平克《人性中的善良天使：暴力为什么会减少》	心理学
An Analysis of Stanley Milgram's *Obedience to Authority*	解析斯坦利·米尔格拉姆《对权威的服从》	心理学
An Analysis of Betty Friedan's *The Feminine Mystique*	解析贝蒂·弗里丹《女性的奥秘》	心理学
An Analysis of David Riesman's *The Lonely Crowd: A Study of the Changing American Character*	解析大卫·理斯曼《孤独的人群：美国人社会性格演变之研究》	社会学
An Analysis of Franz Boas's *Race, Language and Culture*	解析弗朗兹·博厄斯《种族、语言与文化》	社会学
An Analysis of Pierre Bourdieu's *Outline of a Theory of Practice*	解析皮埃尔·布尔迪厄《实践理论大纲》	社会学
An Analysis of Max Weber's *The Protestant Ethic and the Spirit of Capitalism*	解析马克斯·韦伯《新教伦理与资本主义精神》	社会学
An Analysis of Jane Jacobs's *The Death and Life of Great American Cities*	解析简·雅各布斯《美国大城市的死与生》	社会学
An Analysis of C. Wright Mills's *The Sociological Imagination*	解析C.赖特·米尔斯《社会学的想象力》	社会学
An Analysis of Robert E. Lucas Jr.'s *Why Doesn't Capital Flow from Rich to Poor Countries?*	解析小罗伯特·E.卢卡斯《为何资本不从富国流向穷国？》	社会学

An Analysis of Émile Durkheim's *On Suicide*	解析埃米尔·迪尔凯姆《自杀论》	社会学
An Analysis of Eric Hoffer's *The True Believer: Thoughts on the Nature of Mass Movements*	解析埃里克·霍弗《狂热分子：群众运动圣经》	社会学
An Analysis of Jared M. Diamond's *Collapse: How Societies Choose to Fail or Survive*	解析贾雷德·M.戴蒙德《大崩溃：社会如何选择兴亡》	社会学
An Analysis of Michel Foucault's *The History of Sexuality Vol. 1: The Will to Knowledge*	解析米歇尔·福柯《性史（第一卷）：求知意志》	社会学
An Analysis of Michel Foucault's *Discipline and Punish*	解析米歇尔·福柯《规训与惩罚》	社会学
An Analysis of Richard Dawkins's *The Selfish Gene*	解析理查德·道金斯《自私的基因》	社会学
An Analysis of Antonio Gramsci's *Prison Notebooks*	解析安东尼奥·葛兰西《狱中札记》	社会学
An Analysis of Augustine's *Confessions*	解析奥古斯丁《忏悔录》	神学
An Analysis of C. S. Lewis's *The Abolition of Man*	解析 C. S. 路易斯《人之废》	神学

图书在版编目（CIP）数据

解析道格拉斯·麦格雷戈《企业的人性面》：汉、英／斯托扬·斯托扬诺夫，莫妮卡·狄德瑞奇著；童妍译. —上海：上海外语教育出版社，2019
（世界思想宝库钥匙丛书）
ISBN 978-7-5446-5992-5

Ⅰ.①解… Ⅱ.①斯… ②莫… ③童… Ⅲ.①企业管理—人事管理—汉、英 Ⅳ.①F272.92

中国版本图书馆CIP数据核字（2019）第175500号

This Chinese-English bilingual edition of *An Analysis of Douglas McGregor's* The Human Side of Enterprise is published by arrangement with Macat International Limited.
Licensed for sale throughout the world.
本书汉英双语版由Macat国际有限公司授权上海外语教育出版社有限公司出版。
供在全世界范围内发行、销售。

图字：09-2018-549

出版发行：上海外语教育出版社
　　　　　（上海外国语大学内）　邮编：200083
电　　话：021-65425300（总机）
电子邮箱：bookinfo@sflep.com.cn
网　　址：http://www.sflep.com
责任编辑：梁瀚杰

印　　刷：句容市排印厂
开　　本：890×1240　1/32　印张5.125　字数105千字
版　　次：2019年12月第1版　2019年12月第1次印刷
印　　数：2 100册

书　　号：ISBN 978-7-5446-5992-5
定　　价：30.00元
本版图书如有印装质量问题，可向本社调换
质量服务热线：4008-213-263　电子邮箱：editorial@sflep.com